Foreword

I met Vito Radice around thirty five years ago. We were involved in the Humanist Movement at the time and he's been one of my great friends ever since. I would have to say we are like brothers, even though we don't catch up all the time.

He is an incredibly inspirational and worldly person who is amazingly well read and balanced on almost any topic, a person who is always positive and smiling no matter the situation.

He is someone who has a markedly different perspective on life and sees things the majority just do not see. I would venture to say that there are few people around who have a grasp on the joy of life as he does.

Unencumbered by norms and fashions, a free thinker of virtually unlimited scope.

Further, during theses times we met and we're involved in the Humanist movement, which was in itself nothing short of transformational.

Vito was (even 35 years ago), someone who clearly was not one of the sheep or "sheeple", as I call it. He wasn't moved or swayed by the thinking of the time or the current thinking or non-thinking to be more on point.

Even all those years ago, he was a person of bubbling enthusiasm and joy for life and a deep sense of wanting and needing to help others. I was awestruck by it at the time as it was and certainly is now so very rare.

Selfishness and narcissism rule the day at the moment and to have someone who has gone through life and hasn't changed is extraordinary.

I would suggest his bio to be vital reading for anyone who wants to experience spiritual and intellectual growth, emotional liberty and to just pick up some of the puzzle pieces of what makes a human being happy and contented, in what is a very hostile world.

Bob Zaccar

May, 2020

This book is dedicated to my "Family of Friends":
Greg, Brian, Ro and Tree.
"We are NOT blood but we are FAMILY!"
Thank you to Mariclaire, who has been on this grand adventure with me.

— "The Don"

Contents	Page
Chapter 1: In Search of the Meaning in Life	4
Chapter 2: Living in the 1970s...... and 1980s	29
Chapter 3: My Life in a CULT!	39
The Journey Begins	
Chapter 3: The Community for Human Development	50
Chapter 4: The (Great) Escape (from the nest)	77
I gotta get outta of this place!	
Chapter 5: The Humanist Party: Humanise the Earth	81
Chapter 6: The Campaign: Petition for a Referendum to Close Pine Gap 1985-1986	86
Chapter 7: The Elections: 1984-1988	96
Chapter 8: Rise of the Organisms	116
Chapter 9: Crisis! What Crisis? Scorched Earth	136
Chapter 10: The Journey Ends End of the Line	143

To Get in touch with the author

"The Polemicist":
controversial, argumentative, adversarial, agitator, non-conformist, oppositional, enigmatic, agent provocateur, "international man of mystery", trouble-maker, shit-stirrer.

Email: vitoradice@gmail.com
Facebook: Vito Radice
Instagram: don_vito_radice
Website: buonavitabecreative.com
Mobile: 0490 012 461

"Rainy Day Women #12 & 35"

"Well, they'll stone you when you're trying to be so good
They'll stone you just like they said they would
They'll stone you when you're trying to go home
And they'll stone you when you're there all alone
But I would not feel so all alone
Everybody must get stoned

Well, they'll stone you when you're walking on the street
They'll stone you when you're tryin' to keep your seat
They'll stone you when you're walkin' on the floor
They'll stone you when you're walkin' to the door
But I would not feel so all alone
Everybody must get stoned

They'll stone you when you're at the breakfast table
They'll stone you when you are young and able
They'll stone you when you're tryin' to make a buck
Then they'll stone you and then they'll say "good luck"
Tell ya what, I would not feel so all alone
Everybody must get stoned

Well, they'll stone you and say that it's the end
Then they'll stone you and then they'll come back again
They'll stone you when you're riding in your car
They'll stone you when you're playing your guitar
Yes, but I would not feel so all alone
Everybody must get stoned alright

Well, they'll stone you when you walk all alone
They'll stone you when you are walking home
They'll stone you and then say you are brave
They'll stone you when you are set down in your grave
But I would not feel so all alone
Everybody must get stoned"

Performed by : Bob Dyan
Songwriter: Bob Dylan

Chapter 1: In Search of the Meaning in Life

"WAKE UP MY MIND"

I am a man in the prime of my life
I've got a house and a car and a beautiful wife
There's no chip on my shoulder, I've no axe to grind
And no possible reason to Wake Up My Mind.

And the days break and the nights fall and drift into time ...

Somewhere there's hunger, somewhere there's war
But I can do nothing so I'll just ignore
The cruelty around me, pretending I'm blind
In case I start thinking and Wake Up My Mind.

And the days break and the nights fall and drift into time ...

I read in the papers, a policeman shot down
Two negro's in cold blood in some racial town
And I'm having a new car but I don't know what kind
But one of these days I will Wake Up My Mind.

And the days break and the nights fall and drift into time ...

Yes it seems as though fortune has smiled upon me
But now it's too late I'm beginning to see
I've spent my life searching but no peace I find
And it's left me with no time to Wake Up My Mind.

And the days break and the nights fall and drift into time ..."

Performed by: The Ugly's
Songwriters: Burnett, Holden, and Gibbons

What are we here for? What is the purpose of our lives? Is there a meaning or is it all meaningless? A JOKE?

You are born, you struggle and then you die! Without a choice in any of these events!
Struggling, that thing called LIVING, in between being born and dying, is like finding yourself in a rip. All you can do is try to negotiate it as best you can! There is no one to help you!

There is no map.

You are given no skills or techniques to help you.

You are far from land, there are no life guards to signal for help.

There is no point screaming or crying, there is no driftwood to grab on to, to cling on to.

You are all ALONE!

Is our existence just a farce?

Is this a comedy, a musical or a tragedy that we're living in!

Was GOD the answer? And if it was, which GOD? Whose GOD? There were too many Gods! Which one is the RIGHT GOD?

I was raised as a Roman Catholic, so I knew (more or less) about the Christian God but I was NEVER satisfied that it had all the answers for me. I look at people around me who believed in this God and found them to be hypocrites, say one thing and do something completely opposite. My parents for example, especially my father just used God for his own convenience. When things weren't working out for him. He even abused his God, swore at him but then prayed for his help. I was always amazed at his duality, how on one hand he prayed to his God for help but when things were going pear shaped and his prays weren't being answered, or so he thought, he would turn on him. Blame God for looking after him!

These questions vexed and perplexed me.

I went to Drummoyne Boys' High School and there I formed friendships that have lasted to this very day. Almost fifty years later!

These guys are my REAL brothers! My REAL family!

Blood means SHIT!

I was a sensitive teenager! My closest friends from school were also very sensitive. We were not like the other boys at my school. They were into fast, hotted up cars, disco, getting dressed up and looking shmick!

We were intellectuals! Listened to different music: Bob Dylan, Leonard Cohen, Neil Young, Joni Mitchell, Jethro Tull, Led Zeppelin, Pink Floyd and others.

We didn't like cars like the other boys.
We played music.
We wrote stories.
We wrote poetry.
We were artistic.
We valued art.
We took **DRUGS**!

We philosophised.
We went to see plays.
We went to music concerts.
We got drunk.
Some of us had girlfriends.
Some of us had sex.
But not ME!
We got STONED!
We dropped ACID (LSD)!

We were interested in Eastern Philosophies & mystic writing & mysticism in general.
We were interested in Esoteric Writings.
We were interested in Psychology.
We were interested in Religions & Religious Beliefs.
We were interested in Spirituality.
We were interested in Spiritual Enlightenment
We were interested in High Levels of Consciousness.
We were interested in Death & beyond! Is there anything after **Death** or is this *ALL* there is?
We were interested, enquired, studied & sought the *Meaning of Life*!

I was particularly interested in and fascinated in:
The Religious Feeling,
Religiosity,
Altered States,
Psychotherapy,
Cosmology,

Astrology,
Supernatural Phenomena,
Extra-terrestrial Beings.
Surrealism, especially Dali.

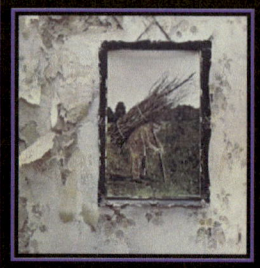

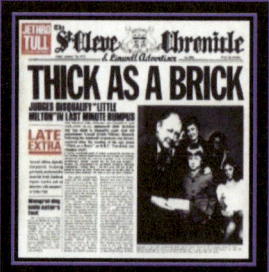

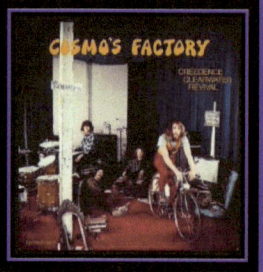

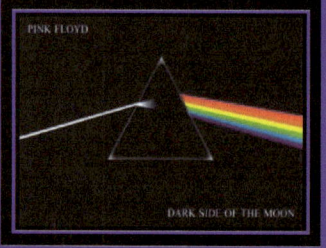

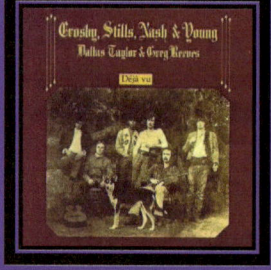
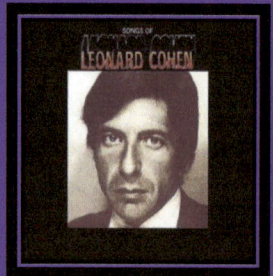
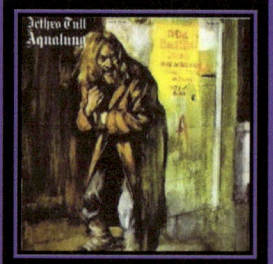

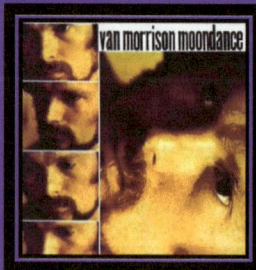

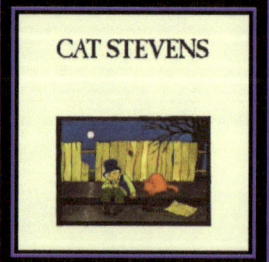

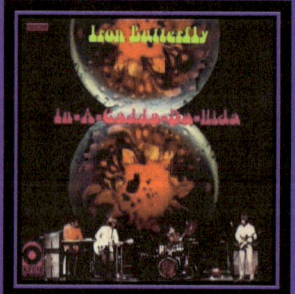

My favourite albums (this page),
My favourite films (next page)

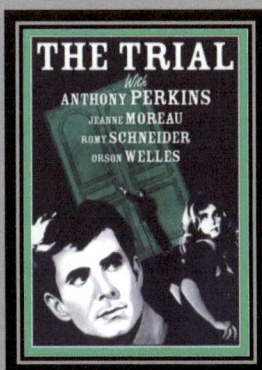
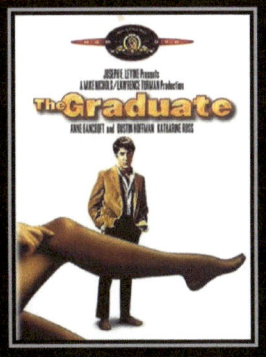

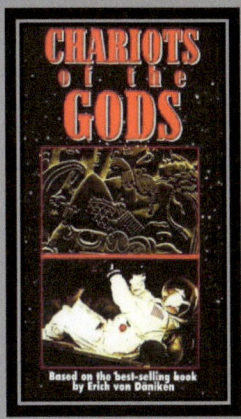

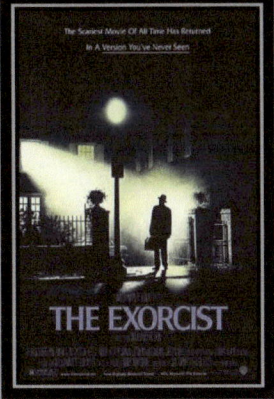

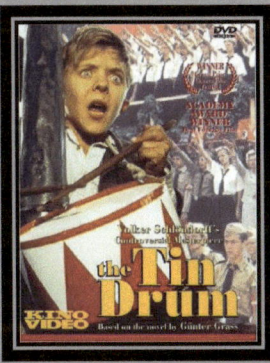

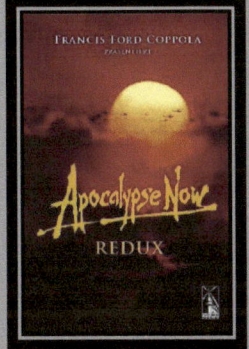

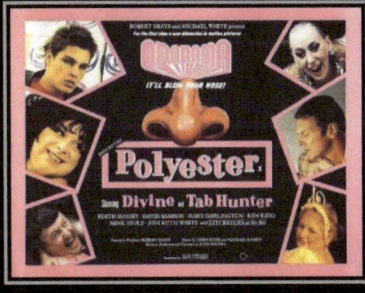

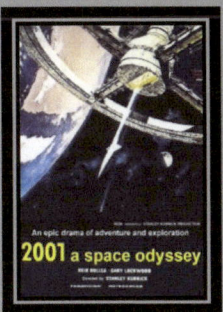

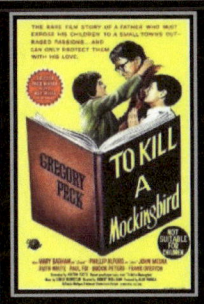
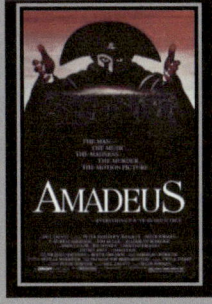

Books and authors that inspired me and influenced my way of thinking and that are still an intrinsic part of my very fabric today (for a variety of reasons) were:

- **Buddha:**
  Siddhārtha Gautama (563/480-c. 483/400 BCE) or *Siddhattha Gotama* in Pali, also called *the Gautama Buddha*, *the Shakyamuni Buddha ("Buddha, Sage of the Shakyas")* or simply *the Buddha*, after the title of *Buddha*, was a *monk*, *mendicant*, *sage*, *philosopher*, *teacher* and *religious leader* on whose teachings *Buddhism* was founded. He is believed to have lived and taught mostly in the north eastern part of ancient India sometime between the 6th and 4th centuries BCE.

  Gautama taught a *"Middle Way"* between sensual indulgence and the severe asceticism found in the *"śramaṇa movement"* common in his region. He later taught throughout other regions of eastern India such as Magadha and Kosala.

  Gautama is the primary figure in *Buddhism*. He is believed by Buddhists to be an *enlightened teacher* who attained full Buddhahood and shared his insights to help sentient beings end rebirth and suffering. Accounts of his life, discourses and monastic rules are believed by Buddhists to have been summarised after his death and memorized by his followers. Various collections of teachings attributed to him were passed down by oral tradition and first committed to writing about 400 years later.

  Buddhism pursues the goal of *overcoming suffering* and the *cycle of death and rebirth* by the attainment of *"Nirvana"*.

  Its methodology is one of *non-violence* and it states that it is not a religion but a philosophy, a way of life, a system of ideas.
  https://en.wikipedia.org/wiki/Gautama_Buddha

- **Hermann Hesse:**
  Hermann Karl Hesse (July 2, 1877-August 9, 1962) was a German-born poet, novelist, and painter. His best-known works include *"Demian"*, *"Steppenwolf"*, *"Siddhartha"*, *"Strange News from Another Star"* and *"The Glass Bead Game"*, each of which explores an individual's search for authenticity, self-knowledge and spirituality.

  In 1946, he received the ***Nobel Prize in Literature***.
  https://en.wikipedia.org/wiki/Hermann_Hesse

- **Franz Kafka:**
Franz Kafka (3 July 1883-3 June 1924) was German speaking Bohemian novelist and short-story writer, widely regarded as one of the major figures of 20th-century literature. His work, which fuses elements of *"realism"* and the *"fantastic"*, typically features isolated protagonists facing bizarre or surrealistic predicaments and incomprehensible socio-bureaucratic powers, and has been interpreted as exploring themes of *alienation*, *existential anxiety*, *guilt*, and *absurdity*. His best known works include "Die Verwandlung" ("The Metamorphosis"), *"Der Process"* (*The Trial*), and *"Das Schloss"* (*The Castle*).

The term *"Kafkaesque"* has entered the English language to describe situations like those found in his writing.
https://en.wikipedia.org/wiki/Franz_Kafka

- **Samuel Coleridge:**
Samuel Taylor Coleridge (21 October 1772-25 July 1834) was an English poet, literary critic, philosopher and theologian who, with his friend **William Wordsworth**, was a founder of the *"Romantic Movement"* in England and a member of the Lake Poets. He also shared volumes and collaborated with Charles Lamb, Robert Southey, and Charles Lloyd.

He wrote the poems *"The Rime of the Ancient Mariner"* and *"Kubla Khan"*, as well as the major prose work *"Biographia Literaria"*.

He helped introduce *"German idealist philosophy"* to English-speaking culture.
Coleridge coined many familiar words and phrases, including *"suspension of disbelief"*.

He had a major influence on **Ralph Waldo Emerson** and on *"American transcendentalism"*.
https://en.wikipedia.org/wiki/Samuel_Taylor_Coleridge

- **Homer:**
(The Odyssey, The Iliad),
Homer is the legendary author of the *"Iliad"* and the *"Odyssey"*, two epic poems that are the central works of ancient Greek literature.

The *"Iliad"* is set during the Trojan War, the ten-year siege of the city of Troy by a coalition of Greek kingdoms.

It focuses on a quarrel between **King Agamemnon** and the warrior Achilles lasting a few weeks during the last year of the war. The *"Odyssey"* focuses on the ten-year journey home of *"Odysseus, king of Ithaca"*, after the fall of *"Troy"*.

Many accounts of Homer's life circulated in classical antiquity, the most widespread being that he was a blind bard from Ionia, a region of central coastal Anatolia in present-day Turkey. Modern scholars consider these accounts legendary.
https://en.wikipedia.org/wiki/Homer

- **The Mahabharata:**
The Mahabharata is an ancient Indian epic where the main story revolves around two branches of a family - the *Pandavas* and *Kauravas* - who, in the *Kurukshetra War*, battle for the throne of *Hastinapura*.

Interwoven into this narrative are several smaller stories about people dead or living, and philosophical discourses.
https://www.ancient.eu/Mahabharata/

- **The Epic of Gigamesh:**
"The Epic of Gilgamesh" tells of the *Sumerian Gilgamesh*, the hero king of *Uruk*, and his adventures.

This epic story was discovered in the ruins of the *library of Ashurbanipal* in *Nineveh* by *Hormuzd Rassam* in 1853.

Written in cuneiform on 12 clay tablets, this *Akkadian* version dates from around 1300 to 1000 B.C.
https://www.historyonthenet.com/the-epic-of-gilgamesh

- **Timothy Leary:**
(October 22, 1920-May 31, 1996) was an American psychologist and writer known for advocating the exploration of the therapeutic potential of *"psychedelic drugs"* under controlled conditions.

Leary believed that *LSD-Lysergic acid diethylamide* showed potential for therapeutic use in psychiatry. He used LSD himself and developed a philosophy of mind expansion and personal truth through LSD. After leaving Harvard, he continued to publicly promote the use of psychedelic drugs and became a well-known figure of the counterculture of the 1960s. He popularized catchphrases that promoted his philosophy, such as:

* *"turn on, tune in, drop out"*,
* *"set and setting"*, and
* *"think for yourself and question authority"*.

He also wrote and spoke frequently about *"transhumanist"* concepts involving *"space migration, intelligence increase, and life extension (SMILE)"*, and developed the eight-circuit model of consciousness in his book *"Exo-Psychology"* (1977). He gave lectures, occasionally billing himself as a *"performing philosopher"*.

During the 1960s and 1970s, he was arrested often enough to see the inside of 36 prisons worldwide. **President Richard Nixon** once described Leary as *"the most dangerous man in America"*.
<https://en.wikipedia.org/wiki/Timothy_Leary>

- **The Tibetan Book of the Dead:**
Commonly known in the West as the *"Tibetan Book of the Dead"*, the *"Bardo Thodol, Liberation Through Hearing During the Intermediate State"* is a text from a larger corpus of teachings, *"The Profound Dharma of Self-Liberation through the Intention of the Peaceful and Wrathful Ones"*, revealed by Karma Lingpa (1326–1386). It is the best-known work of *"Nyingma literature"*.

The Tibetan text describes, and is intended to guide one through, the experiences that the consciousness has after death, in the *"Bardo"*, the interval between death and the next rebirth. The text also includes chapters on the signs of death and rituals to undertake when death is closing in or has taken place.
<https://en.wikipedia.org/wiki/Bardo_Thodol>

- **George Gurdjieff:**
George Ivanovich Gurdjieff (13 January 1866-29 October 1949) was a mystic, philosopher, spiritual teacher, and composer of Armenian and Greek descent, born in *Alexandrapol* (now *Gyumri*), Armenia. Gurdjieff taught that most humans do not possess a unified consciousness and thus live their lives in a state of hypnotic *"waking sleep"*, but that it is possible to awaken to a higher state of consciousness and achieve full human potential.

Gurdjieff described a method attempting to do so, calling the discipline *"The Work"* (connoting *"work on oneself"*) or *"the System"*. According to his principles and instructions, Gurdjieff's method for awakening one's consciousness unites the methods of the *fakir*, *monk* and *yogi*, and thus he referred to it as the *"Fourth Way"*.

In early adulthood, according to his own account, Gurdjieff's curiosity led him to travel to Central Asia, Egypt, Iran, India, Tibet and Rome before he returned to Russia for a few years in 1912. He was always unforthcoming about the source of his teachings.

The only account of his wanderings appears in his book *"Meetings with Remarkable Men"*. Most commentators leave his background unexplained, and it is not generally considered to be a reliable or straightforward autobiography. Each chapter is named after an individual "remarkable man"; many are putatively members of a society of *"seekers of truth"*.
https://en.wikipedia.org/wiki/George_Gurdjieff

- **Gabriel Gibran:**
Gibran Khalil Gibran (commonly known as Khalil Gibran, January 6, 1883-April 10, 1931) was a Lebanese-American writer, poet and visual artist, also considered a philosopher although he himself rejected this title in his lifetime. He is best known as the author of *"The Prophet"*, which was first published in the United States in 1923 and is one of the best-selling books of all time, having been translated into dozens of languages.

His "prodigious body of work" has been described as *"an artistic legacy to people of all nations."*
https://en.wikipedia.org/wiki/Khalil_Gibran

- **Carlos Castaneda:**
Carlos Castaneda (December 25, 1925, April 27, 1998) was an American author.
Starting with *"The Teachings of Don Juan"* in 1968, Castaneda wrote a series of books that describe his training in *"Shamanism"*, particularly with a group whose lineage descended from the Toltecs. The books, narrated in the first person, relate his experiences under the tutelage of a man that Castaneda claimed was a *"Yaqui"*, *"Man of Knowledge"* named *"Don Juan Matus"*.

His twelve books have sold more than 28 million copies in 17 languages. Critics have suggested that they are works of fiction; supporters claim the books are either true or at least valuable works of philosophy.

Castaneda withdrew from public view in 1973, living in a large house in Westwood, California from 1973 until his death in 1998, with three colleagues whom he called *"Fellow Travellers of Awareness."* He founded *"Cleargreen"*, an organization that promotes *"Tensegrity"*, which Castaneda described as the modern version of the *"magical passes"* of the shamans of ancient Mexico.
https://en.wikipedia.org/wiki/Carlos_Castaneda

- **Zen and The Art of Motorcycle Maintenance:**

  "Zen and the Art of Motorcycle Maintenance: An Inquiry into Values (ZAMM)", by Robert M. Pirsig (September 6, 1928-April 24, 2017), is a book that was first published in 1974. It is a work of fictionalized autobiography, and is the first of Pirsig's texts in which he explores his *"Metaphysics of Quality"*.

  The title is an apparent play on the title of the 1948 book *"Zen in the Art of Archery"* by *Eugen Herrigel*. In its introduction, Pirsig explains that, despite its title, *"it should in no way be associated with that great body of factual information relating to orthodox Zen Buddhist practice. It's not very factual on motorcycles, either."*

  Pirsig received a remarkable 126 rejections before an editor finally accepted it for publication and he did so thinking it would never make a bit of profit. Then it was on best-selling lists for decades. Initially, the book sold at least 5 million copies worldwide.
  https://en.wikipedia.org/wiki/Zen_and_the_Art_of_Motorcycle_Maintenance

- **Krishnamurti:**

  Jiddu Krishnamurti (12 May 1895-17 February 1986) was an Indian philosopher, speaker and writer. In his early life he was groomed to be the new *"World Teacher"* but later rejected this mantle and withdrew from the *"Theosophy"* organization behind it.

  His interests included psychological revolution, the nature of mind, meditation, inquiry, human relationships, and bringing about radical change in society. He stressed the need for a revolution in the psyche of every human being and emphasised that such revolution cannot be brought about by any external entity, be it religious, political, or social.

  Krishnamurti was born in India. In early adolescence he had a chance encounter with occultist and theosophist *Charles Webster Leadbeater* on the grounds of the *"Theosophical Society"* headquarters at *Adyar* in Madras. He was subsequently raised under the tutelage of *Annie Besant* and *Leadbeater*, leaders of the Society at the time, who believed him to be a 'vehicle' for an expected *"World Teacher"*. As a young man, he disavowed this idea and dissolved the *"Order of the Star in the East"*, an organisation that had been established to support it.

Krishnamurti said he had no allegiance to any nationality, caste, religion, or philosophy, and spent the rest of his life travelling the world, speaking to large and small groups and individuals. He wrote many books, among them *"The First and Last Freedom"*, *"The Only Revolution"*, and *"Krishnamurti's Notebook"*.
https://en.wikipedia.org/wiki/Jiddu_Krishnamurti

- **Niccolò Machiavelli:**

Niccolò di Bernardo dei Machiavelli (3 May 1469-21 June 1527) was an Italian diplomat, politician, historian, philosopher, writer, playwright and poet of the Renaissance period.

He has often been called the father of modern political philosophy and political science. For many years he served as a senior official in the Florentine Republic with responsibilities in diplomatic and military affairs. He wrote comedies, carnival songs, and poetry. His personal correspondence is of high importance to historians and scholars.

He worked as secretary to the Second Chancery of the Republic of Florence from 1498 to 1512, when the Medici were out of power. He wrote his best-known work *"The Prince" (Il Principe)* in 1513, having been exiled from city affairs.

"Machiavellian" is widely used as a pejorative to characterize unscrupulous politicians of the sort Machiavelli advised most famously in *"The Prince"*. Machiavelli described immoral behaviour, such as dishonesty and the killing of innocents, as being normal and effective in politics. He even encouraged it in many situations. The book gained notoriety due to claims that it teaches *"evil recommendations to tyrants to help them maintain their power"*.

The term *"Machiavellian"* often connotes political deceit, deviousness, and realpolitik. Even though Machiavelli has become most famous for his work on principalities, scholars also give attention to the exhortations in his other works of political philosophy. His much less popular treatise, the *"Discourses on Livy"*, is often said to have paved the way of modern republicanism.

He greatly influenced: *Thomas Hobbes* and *Jean-Jacques Rousseau*.

Quotes:
"It is better to be feared than loved, if you cannot be both."

"Men judge generally more by the eye than by the hand, for everyone can see and few can feel. Everyone sees what you appear to be, few really know what you are."

"The first method for estimating the intelligence of a ruler is to look at the men he has around him."
https://en.wikipedia.org/wiki/Niccol%C3%B2_Machiavelli

- **Albert Camus:**
Albert Camus (7 November 1913-4 January 1960) was a French philosopher, author, and journalist. He won the **Nobel Prize in Literature** at the age of 44 in 1957, the second youngest recipient in history.

Philosophically, Camus's views contributed to the rise of the philosophy known as *"absurdism"*. He is also considered to be an *"existentialist"*, despite his having firmly rejected the term throughout his lifetime.

Camus separated his work into three *"cycles"*. Each cycle consisted of a novel, an essay, and a play.

The first was the cycle of the absurd consisting of *"L'Étranger"* (*The Stranger*), *"Le Mythe de Sysiphe"* (*The Myth of Sisyphus*) and *"Caligula"*.

**(In Greek mythology "Sisyphus" or "Sisyphos" was the king of Ephyra (now known as Corinth). He was punished for his self-aggrandizing craftiness and deceitfulness by being forced to roll an immense boulder up a hill only for it to roll down when it nears the top, repeating this action for eternity.
Through the classical influence on modern culture, tasks that are both laborious and futile are therefore described as "Sisyphean".)**

The second was the cycle of the revolt which included *"La Peste"* (*The Plague*), *"L'Homme révolté"* (*The Rebel*) and *"Les Justes"* (*The Just Assassins*).

The third, the cycle of the love, consisted of *"Nemesis"*.
Each cycle was an examination of a theme with the use of a pagan myth and including biblical motifs.
https://en.wikipedia.org/wiki/Albert_Camus

- **Jack Kerouac:**
Jack Kerouac (March 12, 1922-October 21, 1969) was an American novelist and poet of French-Canadian ancestry.

He is considered a *literary iconoclast* and, alongside *William S. Burroughs* and *Allen Ginsberg*, a pioneer of the *"Beat Generation"*.

Kerouac is recognized for his method of spontaneous prose. Thematically, his work covers topics such as Catholic spirituality, jazz, promiscuity, Buddhism, drugs, poverty, and travel. He became an underground celebrity and, with other beats, a progenitor of the *hippie movement*, although he remained antagonistic toward some of its politically radical elements.

His major works are: *"On the Road"* and *"The Dharma Bums"*.
https://en.wikipedia.org/wiki/Jack_Kerouac

- **Bertrand Russell:**
Bertrand Arthur William Russell (18 May 1872-2 February 1970) was a British philosopher, *logician*, mathematician, historian, writer, essayist, *social critic*, political activist, and *Nobel laureate*. At various points in his life, Russell considered himself a *liberal*, a *socialist* and a *pacifist*, although he also confessed that his sceptical nature had led him to feel that he had "*never been any of these things, in any profound sense.*"

His philosophical essay *"On Denoting"* has been considered a *"paradigm of philosophy"*. His work has had a considerable influence on mathematics, *logic, set theory, linguistics, artificial intelligence, cognitive science, computer science* and *philosophy*, especially the *philosophy of language, epistemology* and *metaphysics*.

Russell was a prominent *anti-war activist* and he championed *anti-imperialism*.

In 1950, Russell was awarded the *Nobel Prize in Literature "in recognition of his varied and significant writings in which he champions humanitarian ideals and freedom of thought"*.
https://en.wikipedia.org/wiki/Bertrand_Russell

- **Fydor Dostovesky:**

Fyodor Mikhailovich Dostoevsky (11 November 1821-9 February 1881), was a Russian novelist, short story writer, essayist, journalist and philosopher.

Dostoevsky's literary works explore *human psychology* in the troubled political, social, and spiritual atmospheres of 19th-century Russia, and engage with a variety of philosophical and religious themes.

His most acclaimed works include *"Crime and Punishment"* (1866), *"The Idiot"* (1869), *"Demons"* (1872), and *"The Brothers Karamazov"* (1880).

His 1864 novella *"Notes from Underground"* is considered to be one of the first works of *existentialist* literature.
https://en.wikipedia.org/wiki/Fyodor_Dostoevsky

- **Aleksandr Solzhenitsyn:**

Aleksandr Isayevich Solzhenitsyn (11 December 1918-3 August 2008) was a Russian novelist, historian, and short story writer.

He was an outspoken critic of the *Soviet Union* and *Communism* and helped to raise global awareness of its *Gulag labor camp system*.

He was allowed to publish only one work in the Soviet Union, *"One Day in the Life of Ivan Denisovich"* (1962), in the periodical *Novy Mir*. After this he had to publish in the West, most notably *"Cancer Ward"* (1968), *"August 1914"* (1971), and *"The Gulag Archipelago"* (1973).

Solzhenitsyn was awarded the *1970 Nobel Prize in Literature "for the ethical force with which he has pursued the indispensable traditions of Russian literature"*.

Solzhenitsyn was afraid to go to Stockholm to receive his award for fear that he would not be allowed to re-enter. He was eventually expelled

from the Soviet Union in 1974, but returned to Russia in 1994 after the state's dissolution.
https://en.wikipedia.org/wiki/Aleksandr_Solzhenitsyn

- **Carl Jung:**
Carl Gustav Jung (26 July 1875-6 June 1961) was a Swiss psychiatrist and psychoanalyst who founded *analytical psychology*.

Jung's work was influential in the fields of *psychiatry, anthropology, archaeology, literature, philosophy*, and *religious studies*.

He conducted a lengthy correspondence and collaborated for a while with *Sigmund Freud, the founder of psychoanalysis*, on a joint vision of *human psychology*.

Among the central concepts of *analytical psychology* is *individuation: the lifelong psychological process of differentiation of the self out of each individual's conscious and unconscious elements*.

Jung considered it to be the main task of human development.

He created some of the best known psychological concepts, including: *synchronicity, archetypal phenomena, the collective unconscious, the psychological complex*, and *extraversion and introversion*.
https://en.wikipedia.org/wiki/Carl_Jung

- **Sigmund Freud:**
Sigmund Freud (born Sigismund Schlomo Freud; 6 May 1856-23 September 1939) was an Austrian neurologist and *the founder of psychoanalysis*, a clinical method for treating psychopathology through dialogue between a patient and a psychoanalyst.

In founding psychoanalysis, Freud developed therapeutic techniques such as: *the use of free association* and *discovered transference*, establishing its central role in the analytic process.

Freud's redefinition of *sexuality* to include its infantile forms led him to formulate the *"Oedipus Complex"* as the central tenet of *psychoanalytical theory*.

His analysis of *dreams* as *wish-fulfillments* provided him with models for the clinical analysis of *symptom formation* and the underlying mechanisms of *repression*. On this basis Freud elaborated his *theory of the unconscious* and went on to develop a *model of psychic structure* comprising *"Id", "Ego"* and *"Super-Ego"*.

Freud postulated the existence of *"The Libido", a sexualised energy with which mental processes and structures are invested and which generates erotic attachments, and a death drive, the source of compulsive repetition, hate, aggression and neurotic guilt.*

In his later works, Freud developed a wide-ranging interpretation and critique of religion and culture.
https://en.wikipedia.org/wiki/Sigmund_Freud

- **Jean-Paul Sartre:**
Jean-Paul Charles Aymard Sartre (21 June 1905-15 April 1980) was a French philosopher, playwright, novelist, screenwriter, political activist, biographer, and literary critic. He was one of the key figures in the philosophy of *existentialism* and *phenomenology*, and one of the leading figures in 20th-century *French philosophy* and *Marxism*.

His work has also influenced *sociology, critical theory, post-colonial theory*, and *literary studies*.

Sartre was also noted for his open relationship with prominent feminist and fellow *existentialist philosopher* and writer *Simone de Beauvoir*.

Together, Sartre and de Beauvior challenged the cultural and social assumptions and expectations of their upbringings, which they considered bourgeois, in both lifestyle and thought. The conflict between *oppressive, spiritually destructive conformity (mauvaise foi*, literally, "*bad faith")* and an "*authentic"* way of "*being"* became the dominant theme of Sartre's early work, a theme embodied in his principal philosophical work *"Being and Nothingness" (L'Être et le Néant)*, 1943.

Sartre's introduction to his philosophy is his work *"Existentialism Is a Humanism" (L'existentialisme est un humanisme)*, 1946, originally presented as a lecture.

In his book *"Sketch for the Theory of Emotions"*, Sartre investigates emotions, describes how they operate in the consciousness and gives a methodology for transforming them. This book was one of the most important books which influenced my understanding of the human consciousness. It gave me a clear understanding and a framework in which to deal with negative situations in daily life.

I highly recommend it, if you are interested in these things!

He was awarded the *1964 Nobel Prize in Literature* despite attempting to refuse it, saying that he always declined official honours and that *"a writer should not allow himself to be turned into an institution"*.
https://en.wikipedia.org/wiki/Jean-Paul_Sartre

- **Isabelle Allende:**
Isabel Allende (August 2, 1942) is a Chilean writer.

Her books are in the genre known as *"Magical Realism"*.

My favourite books are; *"The House of the Spirits" (La casa de los espíritus)*, 1982, *"Of Love and Shadows" (De amor y de sombre)*, 1985 and *"Eva Luna"*, 1987.

Allende has been called *"the world's most widely read Spanish-language author."*

In 2004, Allende was inducted into the American Academy of Arts and Letters, and in 2010, she received *Chile's National Literature Prize*. *President Barack Obama* awarded her the *2014 Presidential Medal of Freedom*.

https://en.wikipedia.org/wiki/Isabel_Allende

- **Eric Von Daniken:**
Erich Anton Paul von Däniken (born 14 April 1935) is a Swiss author of several books which make claims about *extraterrestrial* influences on early human culture.

Von Däniken is one of the main figures responsible for popularizing the *"paleo-contact"* and *ancient astronauts hypotheses*.

The general claim of von Däniken over several published books, is that *extraterrestrials* or *"ancient astronauts"* visited Earth and influenced early human culture. Von Däniken writes about his belief that structures such as the *Egyptian pyramids*, *Stonehenge*, and the *Moai of Easter Island* and artifacts from that period represent higher technological knowledge than is presumed to have existed at the times they were manufactured. He also describes ancient artwork throughout the world as containing depictions of astronauts, air and space vehicles, extraterrestrials, and complex technology.

Von Däniken explains the origins of religions as reactions to contact with an alien race, and offers interpretations of sections of the *Old Testament of the Bible*.

His best-selling book *"Chariots of the Gods?"* was published in 1968.

I loved this book and the subsequent film of the same name. With its controversial subject matter and it's evocative them music and fantastic narrator. It was truly mesmerising. It completely captured my early teenage imagination and was completely hooked! Who can forget that memorable scene in the film of the *"Plains of Nazca"*, in Peru, which shows straight lines dug into the rocky surface that stretch as far as the eyes can see, making absolutely no sense from the surface, BUT if seen from above, from the sky, looking down, from a plane, you see gigantic shapes of spiders, other animals and plants!
https://en.wikipedia.org/wiki/Erich_von_D%C3%A4niken

- **Petrarch:**
Francesco Petrarca (July 20, 1304 – July 18/19, 1374),
commonly anglicized as Petrarch was an Italian scholar and poet and is considered the *"Father of Humanism"*, a philosophy that helped spark the *Italian Renaissance*.

Petrarch's sonnets were admired and imitated throughout Europe during the Renaissance and became a model for lyrical poetry and is considered the father of the modern Italian language..

He is also known for being the first to develop the concept of the *"Dark Ages"*.
https://en.wikipedia.org/wiki/Petrarch

- **Mahatma Ghandi:**
Mohandas Karamchand Gandhi (2 October 1869-30 January 1948) was an Indian lawyer, *anti-colonial nationalist*, and *political ethicist*, who employed *nonviolent resistance* to lead the successful campaign for

India's independence from British Rule, and in turn inspire movements for civil rights and freedom across the world.

Ghandi was assassinated on 30th January 1948 by a Hindu nationalist.

He wrote an amazing autobiography about his life and ideals called, *"Ghandi: An Autobiography: The Story of My Experiences with Truth"*. I highly recommend it.
<https://en.wikipedia.org/wiki/Mahatma_Gandhi>

- **Mario Rodriguez Cobos:**
Mario Luis Rodríguez *Cobos*, also known as *"Silo"* (6 January 1938-16 September 2010), was an Argentine writer and founder of the *"Humanist Movement"*.

An active speaker, he wrote books, short stories, articles and studies related to politics, society, psychology, spirituality and other topics.

Although he described himself simply as a writer, many see him as a thinker, based on the diversity of issues about which he has written.

Cobos studied law for three years at the University of Buenos Aires he began to organize research groups on human beings and their existential and social problems.

On 4 May 1969, *Cobos* spoke to some two hundred people gathered in *Punta de Vacas (Province of Mendoza)*, in the high *Andes mountains* near *Mount Aconcagua*, and gave his first public exposition of the ideas, that in time, would form the basis of the *"Humanist Movement"*. In this talk, known as *"The Healing of Suffering"*, he explained themes such as *the overcoming of pain and suffering, the meaning of life, violence, desire and pleasure.*

In 1972 he published *"The Inner Look"* and the initial groups extended to other countries, partly because the military dictatorships provoked the exile of many of the participants.
In the early 70's, *Cobos* created the current of thought now known as *New Humanism* or *Universalist Humanism*, and founded *"The Humanist Movement"* an organized group that sought to translate this thought into practice.

It can be said that this thinking encompasses the whole of human existence, not only social but also personal.

In 1981 he released *"The Internal Landscape"* and in 1989 he released *"Humanise the Earth"* which included the previous two books and *"The Human Landscape"*.

He was a highly controversial figure until his death, since he was considered a *"spiritual guide"* by his followers, whilst his critics call him a "messianic leader".

He referred to himself as a writer and practitioner of what he called an *"Inner Religion"*.

In a journal of anthropology and American studies, *(Revolución y liberación del ser: apuntes sobre el origen e ideología de un movimiento contracultural esotérico durante el gobierno de Salvador Allende, 1970-1973] en la revista Nuevo Mundo)*, sections of the left began a campaign against *Cobos* and his followers, who were accused of fascism and of being a reactionary movement. At the same time, conservative sectors of the Catholic Church accused them of threatening the family and Christian morality, as seen in the Chilean newspapers of the time. According to *Siloists* this campaign was a reaction to the growing influence of *Cobos* with the young and the proposal of a new *left humanist*, *non-Marxist ideology*.

The notoriety of his influence was reflected in obituaries in the newspapers *Página/12* in Argentina and *El País* in Spain. The latter refers to *Cobos* as the *"founder of a philosophy that came to gather a million followers in over 100 countries"* and *"a strange character for the West, one who could have been born in the East. He trumpeted a spiritual and social change as the foundation of the "human nation""*.

Two months after his death, he was honoured at the Book Fair in *Mar del Plata, Argentina*.
https://en.wikipedia.org/wiki/Mario_Rodr%C3%ADguez_Cobos

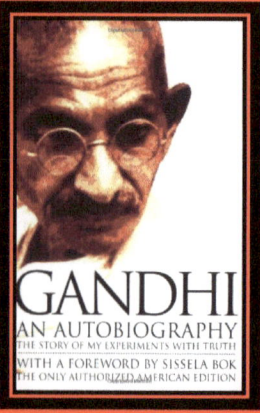
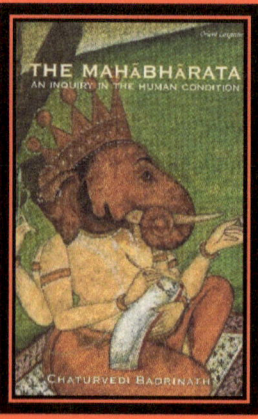
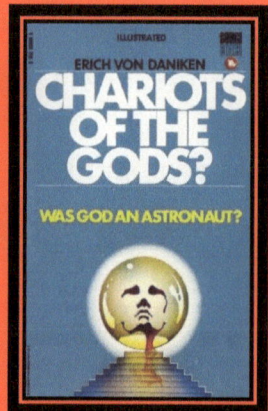
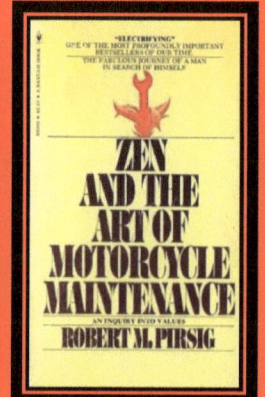
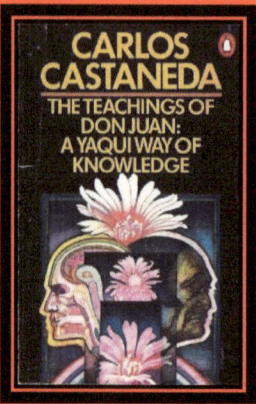

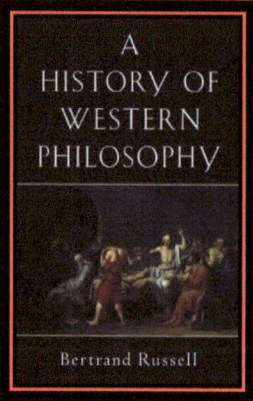
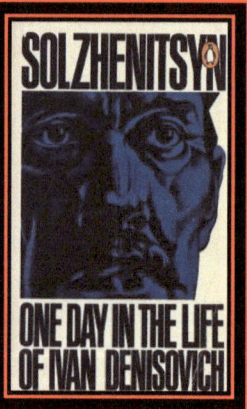

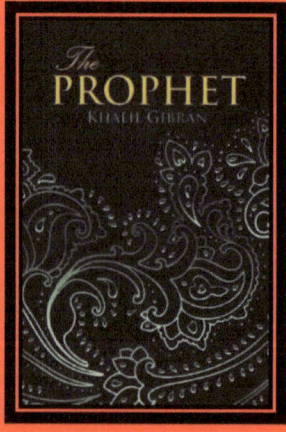

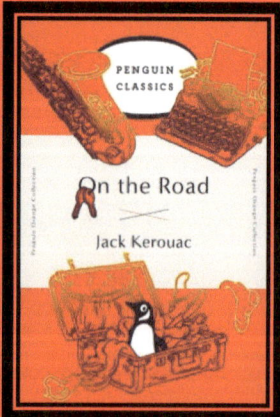
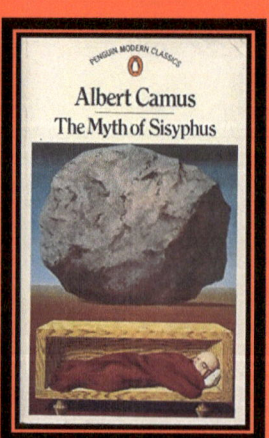

"Question"

"Why do we never get an answer
When we're knocking at the door?
With a thousand million questions
About hate and death and war?
'Cause when we stop and look around us
There is nothing that we need
In a world of persecution
That is burning in its greed

Why do we never get an answer
When we're knocking at the door?
Because the truth is hard to swallow
That's what the war of love is for

It's not the way that you say it
When you do those things to me
It's more the way that you mean it
When you tell me what will be
And when you stop and think about it
You won't believe it's true
That all the love you've been giving
Has all been meant for you

I'm looking for someone to change my life
I'm looking for a miracle in my life
And if you could see what it's done to me
To lose the love I knew
Could safely lead me through

Between the silence of the mountains
And the crashing of the sea
There lies a land I once lived in
And she's waiting there for me
But in the grey of the morning
My mind becomes confused
Between the dead and the sleeping
And the road that I must choose

I'm looking for someone to change my life
I'm looking for a miracle in my life
And if you could see what it's done to me
To lose the love I knew
Could safely lead me to
The land that I once knew
To learn as we grow old
The secrets of our soul
It's not the way that you say it when you do those things to me
It's more the way you really mean it when you tell me what will be

Why do we never get an answer
When we're knocking at the door
With a thousand million questions
About hate and death and war?
When we stop and look around us
There is nothing that we need
In a world of persecution
That is burning in its greed

Why do we never get an answer
When we're knocking at the door?

Performed by: The Moody Blues
Songwriter: Justin Hayward

Chapter 2: Living in the 70s
.... and 80s

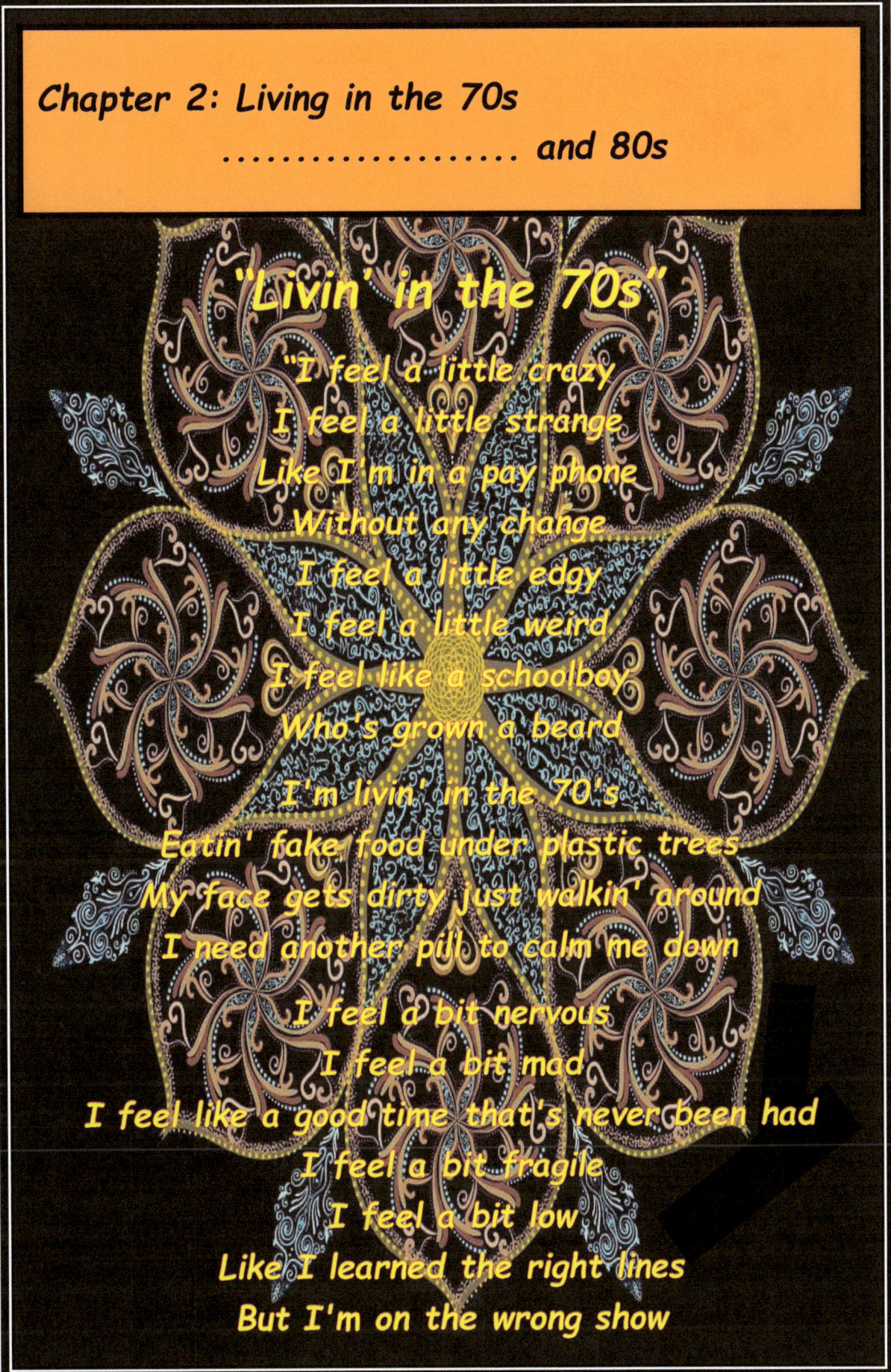

"Livin' in the 70s"

"I feel a little crazy
I feel a little strange
Like I'm in a pay phone
Without any change
I feel a little edgy
I feel a little weird
I feel like a schoolboy
Who's grown a beard

I'm livin' in the 70's
Eatin' fake food under plastic trees
My face gets dirty just walkin' around
I need another pill to calm me down

I feel a bit nervous
I feel a bit mad
I feel like a good time that's never been had
I feel a bit fragile
I feel a bit low
Like I learned the right lines
But I'm on the wrong show

I'm livin' in the 70's
I feel like I lost my keys
Got the right day but I got the wrong week
And I get paid for just bein' a freak

I feel a little insane
I feel a bit dazed
My legs are shrinkin'
And the roof's been raised
I feel a little mixed up
I feel a little queer
I feel like a barman that can't drink a beer

I'm livin' in the 70's
I feel like I lost my keys
Got the right day but I got the wrong week
And I get paid for just bein' a freak"

Performed by: Skyhooks
Songwriter: Gregory J Macainsh

The 1970's were times of great social and political upheaval as Australia, a young nation, an island, no other countries with which to share a land border, a very small population, and an enormous land mass, trying to establish it's identity and place within the community of global nations.

Gough Whitlam and the Australian Labor Party were elected into power and government on 5th December 1972.

Whitlam was elected as PM, with his deputy PM, Lance Barnard, they formed a two-man cabinet and passed a raft of new legislation in the first few days.

They were called *"The Dynamic Duo"*!

They were very well prepared!

New laws passed included:
- *The abolition of conscription* (which up until this stage was compulsory for all males who turned eighteen. They could be drafted and sent to fight in Vietnam, a war in which Australia was involved by supporting the USA).

  My brother, Nick, coincidently had received his draft papers, (he was one of the unlucky chaps chosen out of a ballot to be sent off to fight in Vietnam. He was supposed to leave in February, 1973).

  How lucky was he and many others in the same situation!

- *The legislation to make ALL education FREE*, including tertiary!
- The establishment of *"Medibank"*: free, universal health and medical care for EVERYONE!
- Legislated for *Equal Rights and Pay for women*.
- Recognised *"First Nation's Peoples"* as the original custodians of the nation.

On the 11th November 1975 the greatest upheaval in Australian politics took place: The *Whitlam Labor Government* was dismissed by the *Governor General at the time Sir John Kerr*!

This was an event so massive the like of which Australia have never experienced before or since!
It was so big it rocked the very foundations of our democratic system!

It was the equivalent to a political "nuclear bomb" being dropped onto the Australian political landscape!

It changed EVERYTHING!

The Dismissal of the Whitlam government in 1975 started my interest in politics!

I thought the Dismissal by the Queen to be interference into our sovereignty and to be totally unconstitutional!

The Dismissal had a profound effect on me and my political ideas!

How could a democratically elected government by so trivially and casually dismissed!

What happened to the "Will of the People"?

"The mandate" to government given to it by the people?

The fact that an unelected opposition party (The Liberal Party) was put into power without being elected!

I was shocked and flabbergasted at these events!

I still cannot reconcile these events today, fifty years later!

Since then, Whitlam has become a political cult figure, both revered by "The Left" for his radical reforms, loathed and despised by "The Right' for his very radical & reckless, political agenda! Most criticised his government for (supposedly) mismanagement of the economy, which I do not agree with.

People either loved or hated him!

I loved him!

I loved his intellect, his araldite wit, humour, his love of culture and his love of the ordinary person.

He was a visionary!

An independent Australia free from the shackles of imperialist rule and foreign multinational and Nations!

He gave Australia a new sense of identity, self-worth and belief in itself that it did not have before!

He gave Australia a sense of maturity, a strength to be able to stand on its own on the world stage and not just an appendage of Great Britain!

We even got a new Anthem *"Advance Australia Fair!"*, although a lot thought *"Waltzing Matilda"* captured more of the Australian larrikin spirit!

Whitlam and his government were dismissed at 4:45pm on the 11th November 1975 by The Governor General, the Queen's Representative in Australia (unelected), by a decree from Queen Elizabeth II, the unelected monarch of Australia (most people don't know that Australia is a *"Constitutional Monarchy and NOT a "Republic")!* These words have been cemented into Australia's history:

"Well may we say "God save the Queen", because nothing will save the Governor-General! The Proclamation which you have just heard read by the Governor-General's Official Secretary was countersigned Malcolm Fraser, who will undoubtedly go down in Australian history from Remembrance Day 1975 as Kerr's cur. They won't silence the outskirts of Parliament House, even if the inside has been silenced for a few weeks ... Maintain your rage and enthusiasm for the campaign for the election now to be held and until polling day".

-Gough Whitlam's statement upon his dismal as Prime Minister of Australia
https://en.wikipedia.org/wiki/1975_Australian_constitutional_crisis

Gough Whitlam, Prime Minister (left), Lance Barnard, Deputy Prime Minister and Gough Witlam, 1972

Gough Whitlam, Prime Minister (right), Sir John Kerr, Governor General (bottom), 1975

Malcolm Fraser, *Liberal Party* (conservatives) won the subsequent federal election and a period of austerity followed with lots of funding cuts justified on the previous *Labor Government's* mismanagement of the economy and its inability to reign in foreign debt.

The Labor Party (Democratic Socialist) was re-elected to government under the leadership of Bob Hawke. Hawke was a populist leader with enormous charisma but a big disappointment!

He had a unionist background being a former leader of the ACTU (Australian Council of Trade Unions), the overarching body overseeing all the trade unions in Australia. In this role, he become known as "The Great Communicator" for being able to bring warring parties to conference table and negotiating deals, accords and solutions amicably, in which both parties walked away happy!

However, he was the one who introduced the HECS (Higher Education Contribution Scheme).

I love the use of the word "contribution"!

Tertiary education was No longer FREE!

The thin edge of the edge was introduced and it has gotten worse ever since!

Although he did reintroduce in "Medicare", universal medical care for all which is still the backbone of the health system throughout Australia now!

Paul Keating (treasurer) and Bob Hawke (Prime Minister), 1983

In my late teens, I went to university and started hanging around the inner city, especially Glebe and Newtown. A place that I have extremely fond memories of was *"The Valhalla Cinema"* in Glebe, which has now been converted into apartments. The façade is still there though and when I walk past it now, I get very sad that it is no longer there for others to experience the joy and happiness that I enjoyed.

In the 1980s, it showed 'Art House' films not shown anywhere else. It also had midnight screenings. Many a time was spent with my friends, *"stoned out of our heads"* watching Fellini, John Waters or Andy Warhol films.

Movies that I was inspired by included:

- *"The Tin Drum"* (by *Gunter Grass* an amazing movie and an even more amazing book.)
- *"The Tree of Wooden Clogs"*
- *"Midnight Cowboy"*
- *"Le Grande Bouffe"*
- *"Steppenwolf"*
- *"The Exorcist"*
- *"Star Wars"* (especially the idea of "The Force")
- *"Chariots of the Gods?"* (based on the book by Erik Von Daniken)
- *Koyaanisqatsi* (from the Hopi word meaning *"life out of balance"*)
- *Powaqqatsi*
- *Mondo Cane*
- *A Clockwork Orange*
- *2001: A Space Odyssey*
- *Planet of the Apes*
- *The Bicycle Thief* (Vittorio da Sica; Italian "Neo-Realism" cinema)
- *The Godfather*
- *The Exorcist*
- *Erasurehead*

Albums/songs that I was inspired by included:

- *Blood on the Tracks (Bob Dylan)*
- *Desire (Bob Dylan)*
- *Dirge (Bob Dylan)*
- *Recent Songs (Leonard Cohen)*
- *Songs from the Woods (Jethro Tull)*
- *Aqualung (Jethro Tull)*
- *Thick as a Brick (Jethro Tull)*
- *The Minstrel in the Gallery (Jethro Tull)*
- *Too Old to Rock'n'Roll (But Too Young to Die) (Jethro Tull)*
- *Dark Side of the Moon (Pink Floyd)*
- *Wish You Were Here (Pink Floyd)*
- *The Wall (Pink Floyd)*
- *Led Zeppelin IV (Led Zeppelin)*
- *Dire Straits (Dire Straits)*
- *O Caritas (Cat Stevens)*

- *Age of Aquarius (The 5th Dimension)*

Places that I liked to hang out at included *(though most, sadly, no longer exist)*:

- *The Valhalla*, Glebe
- *The Roxy*, Darlinghurst
- *La Vina*, Leichhardt
- *The Bayview Tavern*, Birkenhead Point, Drummoyne
- *The Pickled Parrot*, Gladesville
- *The Three Weeds (Rose, Shamrock & Thistle)*, Rozelle
- *Haberfield Rowing Club*
- *Drummoyne Rowing Club*
- *Badde Manors*, Glebe

Who could have ever foreseen where all these interests would have led me to and what the future had in store for me and my friends!

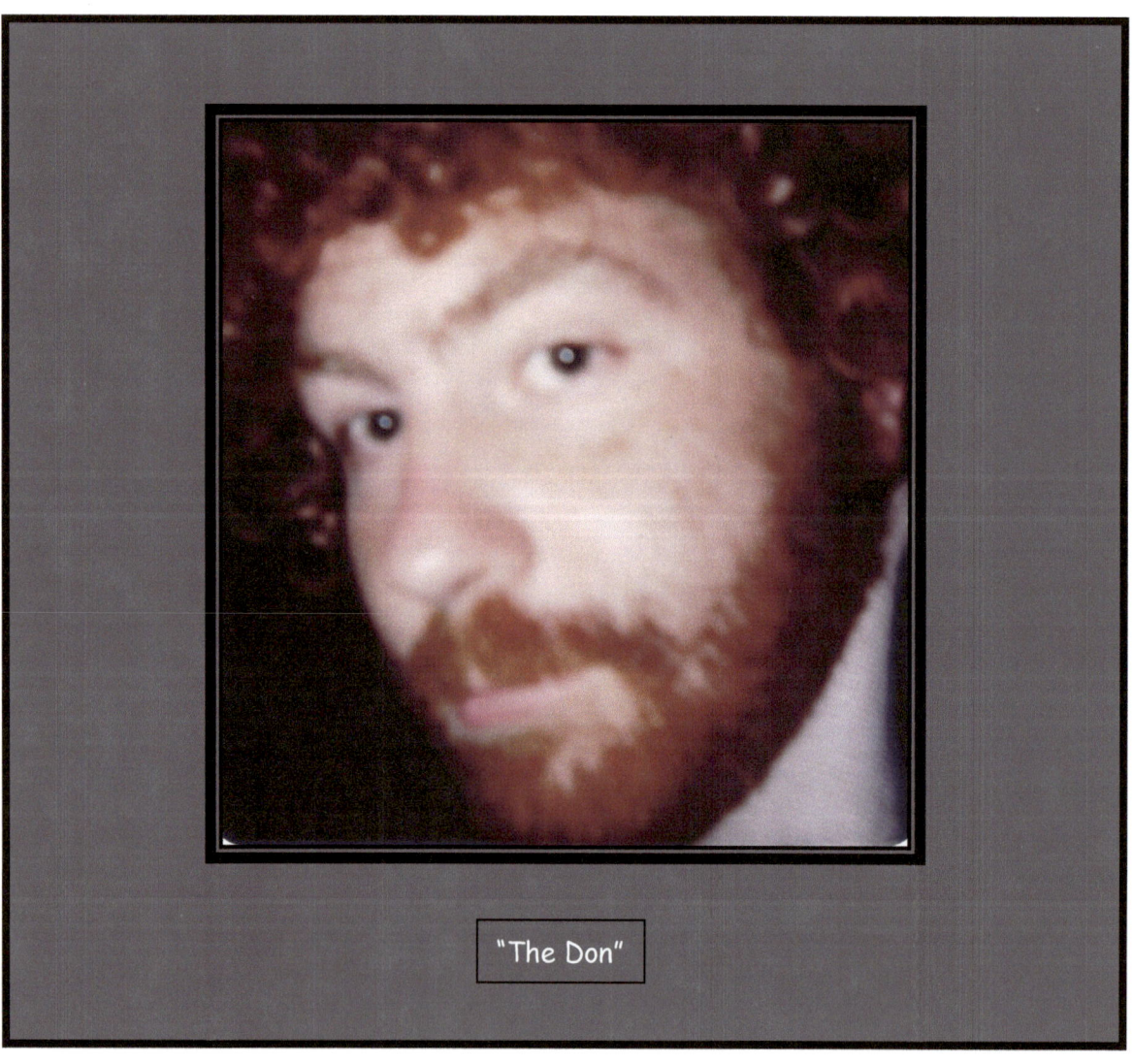

"The Don"

Chapter 3: My Life in a CULT

Lost in a Lost World

I woke today, I was crying
Lost in a lost world
So many people are dying
Lost in a lost world
Some of them are living an illusion
Bounded by the darkness of their minds
In their eyes, it's nation against nation against nation
With racial pride
Sounds...
Thinking only of themselves
They shun the light
(Shun the light)
They think they're right
(Think they're right)
Living in their empty shells

Oh, can you see their bodies thrashing?
(So many people, so many people)
Crashing down around their feet
Angry people in the street
Telling them they've had their fill
Of politics, people who kill

Grow... the seed of evolution
(So many people, so many people)
Revolution everyone
It's just another form of gun
To do again what they have done
Let all our brothers come and get some
(So many people, so many people)

Everywhere you go you see them searching
Everywhere you turn you feel the pain
Everyone is looking for the answers
Well, look again; come on, my friend
Love will find us in the end
Come on, my friend
(On, my friend)
We've got to bend
(Got to bend)
Down on our knees and say a prayer

Oh, can you see the world is pining?
(So many people, so many people)
Pining for someone who really cares enough to share his love
With all of us so we can be
An ever-loving family
Have we forgotten who loves who?
(So many people, so many people)
Children from a family tree
That's longer than a centipede
Started long ago when you and I
Where only love...
(So many people, so many people)

I woke today, I was crying
Lost in a lost world
So many people are dying
Lost in a lost world
So many people, so many people
People lost in a lost world
So many people, so many people
People lost in a lost world"

Performed by: The Moody Blues
Songwriter: Mike Pinder

> **"What is a CULT?":**
>
> *"The term cult has usually been used in reference to a social group that is defined by its unusual religious, spiritual, or philosophical beliefs, or by its common interest in a particular personality, object or goal.*
>
> *This sense of the term is controversial and it has divergent definitions both in popular culture and academia and it has also been an ongoing source of contention among scholars across several fields of study.*
>
> *It is usually considered negative."*
> *https://en.wikipedia.org/wiki/Cult*

I have always been interested and searched for *"The Meaning of Life"* and so may come as no surprise that on particular day my friend Greg introduced me to **"The Community for Human Development"**.

We had both taken the day off from I from *"Kenso Kindy"*, *NSW University* and Greg from *Sydney University*.

We were in my bedroom *"chewing the fat"*, discussing existential ideas *(basically wanking on, as seemingly so called, pseudo intellectual teenage boys do)*, when he says that he had had an amazing experience and if I was interested to experience it as well. He said that he had done a *"Guided Experience"* carried out by another mutual school friend ours Phil.

All I had to do was lay back on my bed, close my eyes, relax and follow the story that the narrated. (Greg had an amazing memory).

His memory abilities were astonishing!

He could remember every word and verse of many very long *Bob Dylan*, *Leonard Cohen* and *Arlo Guthrie* songs such as;
- *"Mr Tambourine Man"*,
- *"Idiot Wind"*,
- *"Tangled Up in Blue"*,
- *"Stuck Inside a Mobile with the Memphis Blues Again"*,
- *"The Ballad of Frankie Lee & Judas Priest"*,

- *"Lily, Rosemary & the Jack of Hearts"*,
- *"Suzanne"*,
- *"Famous Blue Raincoat"*,
- *"Chelsea Hotel"*,
- *"So Long, Marianne"*,
- *"Alice's Restaurant"*,
- *"The Motorcycle Song"* and so many others.

So it was no surprise that he could remember it word for word, in its entirety!

It was called **"The Journey"**!

The Journey*

I'm climbing along a mountain path, and stop briefly to look behind me. In the distance I see the thin line of a river and what could be a grove of trees. Farther off, the reddish desert disappears into the haze of the late afternoon.

I walk a few more steps, and the path narrows until it disappears. I know that I still have the last and most difficult stretch ahead of me before I reach the plateau on top. The snow on the ground scarcely hinders my steps, and I continue my ascent.

I come to a rock wall. Studying it carefully, I discover a large crevice that I think I can climb. I begin to climb it, wedging my hiking boots into the footholds. Pressing my back against one side, I lever myself up with one elbow and my other arm. Slowly I inch higher.

Now the crevice has narrowed. I look up and I look down. I've reached an impasse—it's impossible to move in either direction.

I shift my position, flattening myself against the slippery rock face. Planting both feet firmly, I slowly stretch one arm upward. I can feel my moist breath reflecting from the smooth rock. I keep groping with my fingers, not knowing whether I'll find some small handhold. Gingerly I stretch out my other arm. Suddenly I feel myself swaying, and my head falls slowly away from the rock. My whole body follows, until I'm on the verge of falling backwards—but at the last second, I find a tiny crack and grasp it tightly with my fingers. Recovering my balance. I continue the ascent, making the final assault on the top without difficulty.

At last I reach the plateau. I stand up, and an endless prairie stretches before me. Taking a few steps forward I turn around. Toward the abyss it is already night. Toward the plain the last rays of the sun escape in varied hues. As I compare these two spaces, suddenly I hear a piercing sound. Looking up, I see a luminous disk hovering high overhead. Circling around, it begins to descend.

The disk lands close by. Moved by some inner call, I approach it without hesitation. As I enter the luminous object, it feels as if I'm passing through a curtain of warm air. I find myself inside a transparent bubble that's flattened on its base, and immediately my body feels lighter.

As though propelled by a giant slingshot, we shoot straight upward into the sky. I think we're heading toward the star Beta Hydris, or perhaps the galaxy NGC 3621.

Fleetingly I see the late afternoon light on the prairie below. We climb at great speed as the sky turns black and the Earth slips away.

I can feel our velocity steadily increasing, and the clear white light of the stars changed colour until all the stars have disappeared in total darkness.

Directly ahead I see a single point of golden light, which steadily grows larger. As we approach, I see it is a vast ring that continues into a very long transparent tube. We enter the tube, and after a while come to a sudden stop, landing in an open area. Passing through the curtain of warm air, I leave the bubble.

I find myself between transparent walls, which shimmer in musical variations of color as I pass through them.

I walk onward until I come to a flat area. In the center I see a large object, alive with movement, and impossible to capture with my eye as it flows endlessly into itself; regardless of which direction I look on its surface, my gaze always ends up immersed, drawn deep into the object's interior. Feeling dizzy, I look away.

Now I encounter a figure, apparently human, whose face I cannot see. This being extends a hand toward me, in which I see a radiant sphere. I begin to approach, and in an act of complete acceptance, I take the sphere and place it on my forehead.

> *In total silence I feel something new coming to life within me. A growing force bathes my body in successive waves as a profound joy fills my being.*
>
> *Somehow I know that even without words this figure is speaking to me, saying, "Return to the world with your forehead and your hands luminous."*
>
> *And so I accept my destiny, returning to the bubble, and through the vast ring to the stars, and the prairie, and the rock wall below.*
>
> *Finally, I am back on the mountain path, a humble pilgrim returning to my people.*
>
> *Filled with light, I return to the hours, to the daily routine, to the pain of humanity, and to its simple joys.*
>
> *I, who give with my hands what I can, who receive both insults and the warmest of greetings, sing to the heart, which from the darkest abyss is reborn in the light of Meaning.*
>
> **Sometimes called "The Voyage"*
>
> *Written by: Mario Rodriguez Cobos*
>
> http://www.silo.net/en/collected_works/guided_experiences

It BLEW my mind!

I had NEVER had such a MIND BLOWING experience before!

Greg asked if I had liked it?

"It was like having a trip!", I said.

He said that there was a group that did this stuff and they called it doing *"Internal Work"* and this, was called a *"Guided Experience"*. The next meeting was on Friday night, 7:30pm at Kirribilli Neighbourhood Centre, if I was interested in going along. I said sure, why not?

So off, I went on that Friday night.

Kirribilli Neighbourhood Centre is a very impressive Victorian mansion with a bullnose, wrap-around verandah, set amidst a beautiful garden, overlooking The

Sydney Opera House and The Sydney Harbour Bridge. You couldn't get a more picturesque or beautiful setting even if you could imagine it!

It was raining!

I LOVE rain! Especially rainy nights!

The room was at the front of the building, the first door to your left as you entered the corridor facing a staircase which led to the upstairs floor. I entered the room. It was a large room with its walls and ceiling painted white and a bay window facing the street. A group of about twenty people were sitting in a circle in the middle of the room. I sat on a chair.

It was explained by a person (all in white), running the meeting that we were going to do some *"Internal Work"*, which would include a *"relaxation"*, a *"Guided Experience"*, called *"Death"* and afterwards *"discussion of our experiences"*. He asked everyone to close our eyes and follow what he was reading.

It was a totally new experience for me. I really enjoyed it! It felt light and euphoric.

After the meeting my friends and I remained talking and we were invited to continue our discussions at his place, which was an apartment just down the road. So, we all walked out into the rainy, windy night following him to his apartment.

There was something surreal and mystical that night!

A raining, windy night and the street lights and the dark, the shadows, the reflections, the glare, with you best friends, the view of the Sydney Opera House in front, going off to a complete stranger's apartment.

It was an ***ADVENTURE!***

The building was an old, brown brick "Art Deco" place and he lived in a one bed room apartment on the top floor. It had little furniture and so we all sat on the carpeted floor.

We talked for what seemed an eternity. Finally, we decided to leave at about 11:00pm.

It was still raining!

I was HOOKED!

The person's name was ***Nestor Valenzuela***.

The group was called *"The Community for Human Development"*!

Death

I know I am dying. Scenes from different moments of my life flash before me with the speed of lightning. I also see totally new landscapes and I hear sounds and words that are not in my memories. I can understand that these landscapes and sounds are my own moods: dark emotions that take me to grey chambers, to deep abysses, to heavy sounds, to faraway landslides. And when hope sparkles, the green prairies stretch onward infinitely, and the sounds are hymns and kind words.

There, my body is lying faraway and still. But how can I see and listen and remember and imagine, if I am separated from what once were my senses, from what was my brain, my pulse, my life giving breath?

In this confusion of spaces and times, I stay very close to my body. In this way, when I see dark labyrinths, I am inside my body; when I climb golden mountains, I feel my head in repose. The high, the low, the deep; everything that happened and everything I believe will happen, all have my body as the middle point. Everything that keeps me attached is the past, just as the shadow is attached to a body, without being a body.

Perhaps, because of this, I am attached to the cruel moments of my life: to the frustrations, to the resentments, to the revenge...as if these were solid objects that block the light away from me. When there are no objects, the light shines fully and there is no shadow and this is only possible if my memories have neither frustration, nor resentment, nor revenge, to stop the flow of light. Otherwise, they will stay here, trying to resolve what cannot be resolved.

Hence, life is the means that the mind uses to tear this net of shadows. I am thankful for having known the only important thing: to act with unity. I am thankful for having understood that life has a faraway meaning, a meaning that does not become exhausted by the absurdity of life itself. I am thankful for having guided my actions with my gaze always set in the direction of this meaning.

I feel compassion for those left behind, trapped in the net of shadows, believing that their little illusions are the only truth. Can someone or something ever free them?

I feel compassion for those whom the message of liberation reached, but degraded it, because in their day their confusion will be enormous, unlike those who gave meaning to their lives, and also unlike those who have never known the message and yet acted with internal unity... because they, too, will arrive at the Light.

But now is the triumphant moment of my liberation, and I follow the images that my Guide translates into these words:

"On the inner road, you may walk darkened or luminous. Attend to the two ways that unfold before you."

"If you let your being hurl itself towards dark regions, your body wins the battle and dominates. Then, sensations and appearances of spirits, of forces, of remembrances, will arise. This way, you descend more and more. Here dwell Hatred, Vengeance, Strangeness, Possession, Jealousy, and Desire to Remain. If you descend even further, you will be invaded by Frustration, Resentment, and all those reveries and desires that have brought ruin and death upon humanity."

"If you impel your being toward the light, you will find resistance and fatigue at each step. Your life weighs, your memories weigh, your previous actions impede the ascent. The climb is made difficult by the action of your body which tends to dominate."

"In the steps of the ascent you will find strange regions of pure colours and unknown sounds."

"Do not flee the purification which acts like fire horrifies with its phantoms."

"Reject startling fears and disheartenment."

"Reject the desire to flee towards low and dark regions."

"Reject the attachment to memories."

"Remain in internal liberty, with indifference toward the dream of the landscape, with resolution in the ascent."

"The pure light dawns in the summits of the great mountain chain and the waters of the-thousand-colours flow among unrecognisable melodies towards crystalline plateaus and pastures."

"Do not fear the pressure of the light that moves you further from its centre, each time with increasing strength. Absorb it as though it were a liquid or a wind. Certainly, in it is life."

"When you find the hidden city in the great mountain chain, you must know the entrance. But you will know this in the moment in which your life is transformed. Its enormous walls are written in figures, are written in colours, are "felt". In this city are kept the done, and to be done... But for your inner eye, the transparent is opaque."

Thus speaks my Guide. I prepare myself to do so and everything becomes transparent, and I become liberated from all ties... I am reconciled, I am purified. I am going to the city of Light, that city never perceived by the eye, whose singing has never been heard by human ears.

...I feel that I am stopping, and that I am coming back to my body. My heart beats, my lungs work. Here I am again. But I know that this truth I was able to touch, will act sooner or later, converting the meaning of my life.

Written by: Mario Rodriguez Cobos
http://www.silo.net/en/collected_works/guided_experiences

Chapter 4: The Community for Human Development
(The Community for the Equilibrium & Development of the Human Being)

A Song of Joy

Come sing a song of joy for peace shall come, my brother
Sing, sing a song of joy for men shall love each other.
That day will dawn just as sure as hearts that are pure,
Are hearts set free. No man must stand alone
With outstretched hand before him.

Reach out and take them in yours with love
That endures forevermore. Then sing a song of joy
For love and understanding.

Es cu-cha her-ma-no la can-cion de la a-le-gri-a
El can-toa-le-gre del que es-pe-ra un nue-vo di -a
Ven can-ta sue-na can-tan-do vi-ve so-nan-do el nue-vo sol
En que los hombres vol-ve-ran a ser her-ma-nos

Sien tu ca-mi-no so-lo existe la triste za
Yel llan-to a-mar-go de la so le dad com-ple-ta
Ven canta sue-na can-tan-do vive so-nan-do el nue-voe sol
En que los hombres vol-ve-ran a ser her-man-nos

Come sing a song of joy of freedom tell the story.
Sing, sing a song of joy for mankind in his glory.
One mighty voice that will bring a sound
That will ring forevermore.
Then sing a song of joy for love and understanding.

Come sing a song of joy of freedom tell the story.
Sing, sing a song of joy for mankind in his glory.
One mighty voice that will bring a sound
That will ring forevermore.

Performed by: Miguel Rios
Songwriters: Billy Preston/Rasputin Boutte

Spirits in the Material World

"There is no political solution
To our troubled evolution
Have no faith in constitution
There is no bloody revolution

We are spirits in the material world
Are spirits in the material world
Are spirits in the material world
Are spirits in the material world

Our so-called leaders speak
With words they try to jail you
They subjugate the meek
But it's the rhetoric of failure

We are spirits in the material world
Are spirits in the material world
Are spirits in the material world
Are spirits in the material world

Where does the answer lie?
Living from day to day
If it's something we can't buy
There must be another way

We are spirits in the material world
Are spirits in the material world
Are spirits in the material world
Are spirits in the material world
Are spirits in the material world
Are spirits in the material world."

Songwriter: Sting
Performed by: The Police

Nestor was in his late twenties, short, quite charismatic, always wore white or beige clothes, from Santiago, Chile and had brought *"The Community"* with him to Sydney, Australia in about 1978. He had become involved in Chile, a couple of years earlier. He started running meetings all around Sydney, usually hiring rooms in Neighbourhood centres. Phillip saw a poster on a wall at Sydney University where he was attending. The poster simply stated, *"In Search of the Meaning in Life"*, this caught Phil's attention and he decided to attend the lunchtime meeting.

This is how my group of friends become involved.

Most of my friends became involved, to a greater or lesser degree.

In the early days, the meetings involved carrying out *"Internal Work"*, doing "Guided Experiences", which Nestor had photocopies *(it was not until 1980 that a book called, "The Book of Community" was published)* and later after the meetings go back to his place where we would continue the discussions and Nestor would tell us more about *"The Community"* and stories of *Cobos*.

"Power, sex or money" are the three motivating reasons a person does something, *Nestor* used to often say.

Nestor explained that there was a *"Structure"* and a mechanism called *"Lines"* and that we were connected through him to *"Tito's Line"*, who lived in Tokyo, Japan.

Apparently, in the early days when *"The Community"* was being formed, *Cobos*, the founder had formed a team of people with whom he took away from society into the mountains of Argentina, where they carried out intense "Internal Work". They were asked to leave their families, friends, jobs, studies and devout themselves to the studies of *"Self-Awareness"*. This they did for a couple years. When *Cobos* thought they were ready, these people were sent on *"Missions"* to different parts of the globe to build *"The Community"*.
The places that they were sent to, that I know of were, Japan, USA, Sri Lanka, Canada, Iceland and Spain.

Nestor was NOT a part of this team and he was not sent here on a mission nor was he ever a part of *Cobos'* inner circle.

In those early days all we did was "Internal Work", which we loved. In weekly meetings and weekend retreats, more intensive work from a book called *"Self-Liberation"* written by *Luis A. Amman* was carried out.

I loved this!

One my favourite places where we would go for a weekend retreat was called *"Ahmisa" ("hut-happy-omen")* in Cheltenham *(I wonder if it is still available today? I guess I'll have to "Google" it!)*. It was an open, one room hut, in a bushland setting, hired from *"NSW Parks and Wildlife"*, available for non-profit organisations to use.

Other places we used were:

- Woodstock Neighbourhood Centre, Burwood
- Annandale Neighbourhood Centre, Annandale
- Surry Hills Neighbourhood Centre, Surry Hills
- Summer Hill Community Centre, Summer Hill
- Bondi Beach Community Centre, Bondi Beach
- Drummoyne Community Centre, Drummoyne
- A member's holiday cottage, high on a cliff, overlooking the beach at Queenscliff
- Newtown Neighbourhood Centre, Newtown Locale
- Rozelle Neighbourhood Centre, Rozelle
- Gladesville Neighbourhood Centre, Gladesville
- Chatswood Neighbourhood Centre, Chatswood
- Lavender Bay Neighbourhood Centre, North Sydney
- Bankstown Community Centre, Bankstown
- Kings Cross, Locale
- Stanmore, Locale

One very important person who arrived from Germany in 1980 is *Angelika*. I was attracted and mesmerised by her as soon as I saw her. She was like an *"Amazonian Warrior"*. Strong, opinionated, fearless and very sexy!

She shared a house in Balmain at this time with another member called *Nicola*, who had just arrived from Italy. Later on that year she would marry *Nestor* and the moved into a place on King Street, Newtown which had a shop front and this was used as a *"Locale"* (meeting place). They lived upstairs and the *"Locale"* was used for meetings.

It was a fantastic place!

One of most treasured memories and unforgettable experiences was a one week retreat that I went to in *Sri Lanka* 1981 with another member called *Daniel*.

There were about fourteen other members from and run by a guy called *Julian*. It took place in a very remote part at a place called "World's End"!

This was an amazing location. It was a very remote inaccessible place, high in the mountains and to get there we had to travel along a very steep, windy, narrow dirty road. The road was treacherous and perilous. It was not wide enough for two cars, let alone big trucks and many times we almost on the very edge of the road. Below us was a steep ravine. A fall from here would have certainly meant a lot of injuries, if not death. It was very scary but also very exciting. We went there in a mini bus, all the members travelling together and it took a couple of hours to get to the summit.

Once there we were greeted by amazing views of the mountains and the valley below, that stretched out forever before us. We were literally *"above the clouds"*.

It is 1,067 metres above sea level with a 300 metre vertical drop.

The place was an old colonial estate house complete with outhouses and other nooks and crannies. It is only about 500 metres, a short walk away, through a forest, which took about fifteen minutes by foot! Locals told us that there were tigers and snakes in there but I didn't encounter any. Maybe they were just jungle myths to excite and scare the tourists!

This was really *"Heaven"*!

It is now a guest house called *"Hatale Mini World's End Bungalow"*.

I could not tell my parents I was going off to Sri Lanka for ten days, so I told them I was going to *Surfers' Paradise, Queensland* with some friends instead.

Another memorable weekend retreat was held in a beach house in Kilcare, Central Coast. We arrived late on a Friday night driving up from Sydney. It was cold, raining and windy, a perfect scenario for *"Internal Work"*!

You know how I love this sort of weather!

It was right on the beach.

An awesome place!

Other retreats were held at Lane Cove River Park, Lane Cove, in the convention centre. A bushland setting in the heart of suburbia!

A weeklong retreat was held in Como, high in the mountain country. It was summer time (early January) and very hot during the day but very cold at night. It was a sprawling chalet (probably designed for the snow season), it had a huge open fireplace around which you could sit. It was fantastic!
These were my favourite times!

From top L-R, Locale on Kings St., Newtown, Symbols, retreat at Lane Cove River Park

From top L-R, Vito, Vito, Greg and Tree at Surry Hills Neighbourhood Centre, 21st September, 1981

From top L-R, Vito, Vito, Nestor, Vito, at a rally, (Centre) at a march, (Bottom 4) Ahimsa

Retreat at World's End, Sri Lanka, 1981

A group photo of all who participated in the retreat.
Daniel and I are at the front left. Sherwin is second from the right.

The building of friendships, sharing experiences, discussing ideas, forming new relationships, reconnecting with old friendships, eating, singing and learning together!

A real community of fellow human beings together on the same adventure, same journey!

The Symbol of *"The Community"* was an equilateral triangle with its apices touching the perimeter, inside a circle with an orange background. Apparently, the colour orange represents *"SERVICE"* and the three apices of the triangle represent *Peace*, *Force* and *Joy* a greeting which was accompanied with the *"Hand Symbol"* of the *thumb*, *index* and *middle* fingers *(just like the "Peace Sign" but with the thumb added)* used when greeting and saying goodbye to a fellow member.

Later on, it also became to represent: Structure, Support and Administration. The circle represented *"The Whole"*.

We ran Community meetings in Bondi Beach in the *"Craft Room"* of the Bondi Beach Pavilion.

What a location!

The *"Craft Room"* was a long narrow room, on the inside of the Pavilion. The Pavilion had an open, outdoor theatre, in the middle of it. It was an open quadrangle.

We were chronic smokers and on one particular night we smoked so many cigarettes that the room became completely full of smoke. One new person, after the meeting said that she really loved the ideas but would not be returning because we smoked too much!

I thought it was mandatory to smoke, if one was to be an intellectual and a revolutionary!

It was on a cold and wintery, Wednesday night, after a Community meeting, in Bondi. Phil, Greg and I decided to go to *"The Cross"* (Kings Cross), the notorious red light district of Sydney. It has now become gentrified but back in my day it was it was sleazy and notorious. Some would say that it was bad and needed to change!

I, on the other hand, loved it. Loved its personality, its characters, its venues and the night life, which now has ALL gone.

Kings Cross is no longer the *Kings Cross* of my youth, in the 1980s and 90s. Now, it has become gentrified and acceptable.

With the enormous urban development going on and the introduction of the *"lock-out"* laws, Sydney has lost its vibrancy, culture, venues, it's LIFE!

One of my favourite places where I used to be a regular in *"The Cross"* was the *"Manzil Room"*, (it was located at 15 Springfield avenue and operated until 1990, when the venue changed its name to *"Springfields"*). It no longer exists, like so many places. But it still lives on in my memory. This place was not a place for *"lock-out"* laws. It didn't open its doors until 11:00pm. It had live bands playing but they didn't get on stage till 1:00am or 2:00am. So this was not a place for an early night, more like an early morning! Say 6am or 7am in the morning.

Here we were outside a brothel to pick up a prostitute!

We walked into a brothel and all the girls we sitting watching TV. We didn't know what was going on. They all seemed to be very excited at what was happening. We asked them what was going on and one of the girls told us it was the wedding of the century!

Prince Charles was marrying Lady Diana Spencer!
I couldn't believe it!

Here we were going to get a screw on the night of this momentous, world-wide event!

It seemed serendipitous!

We each chose a girl, although they seemed reluctant to leave the ceremony!
I was led through a corridor, up some stairs, into a very small dark room, no bigger than a shoebox.

She said it was $40 for a fuck and $20 for a blowjob. I said I'll have a fuck please and gave her the money. She fell on the bed, still with her clothes on and said, *"Come on get it in!"*.

I knew at this point that this was not going to go well.
I got on top of her, both still clothed, and I pulled my dick out of my pants. She lay beneath me completely motionless. Which was very off putting. I tried to get an erection but try as I might, I could not.

After a while she said, "Is it in yet?".

By this stage I knew I had FAILED!

I got off her, zipped up my pants and said I was done and walked out.

I was not a pleasurable or pleasant experience!

Afterwards, outside back on the wintery streets of Kings Cross when the others asked me how it was, I said it was FANTASTIC!
How could I tell them the truth?

Later on I realised she was as high as a kite. Poor thing didn't have a clue what was going on!

This was my first sexual experience 29th July, 1981.

I was twenty two years old!

The Community had two parts to it: the *"Internal Work"* and the *"Structural work"*.

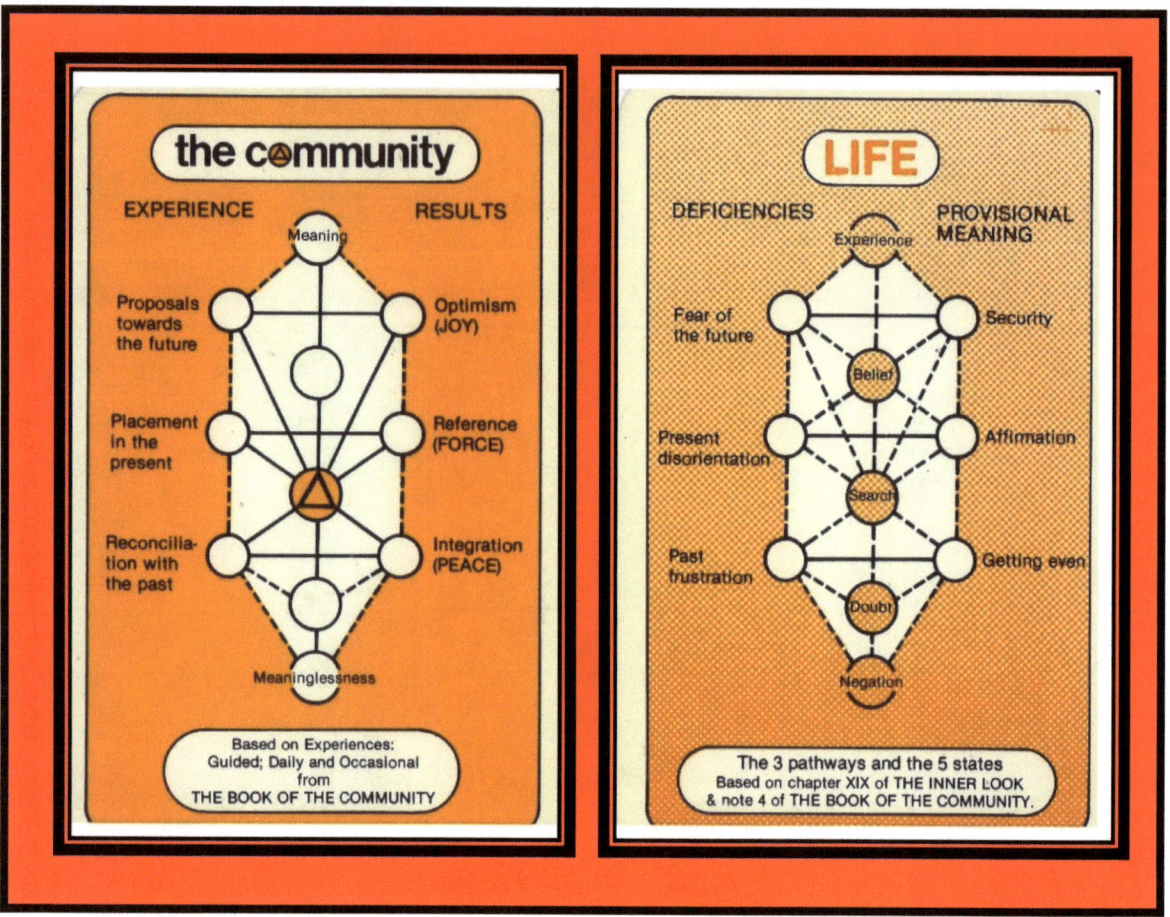

The Internal Work:

This was about *"Self-development"* and was what initially attracted myself *(and other people in general)* to it and was what I *(and most people)*, found easy to understand.

The materials included:
- *"The Healing of Suffering"*, Mario Rodrigues **Cobos** (States the three pathways of suffering),
- *"The Look Within (The Inner Look)"*, Mario Rodrigues **Cobos** (States that the search for the meaning of life is an internal one),
- *"The Internal Landscape"*, Mario Rodrigues **Cobos** (The objective is to move freely within one's Internal Landscape and not to get stuck),
- *"The Human Landscape"*- Mario Rodrigues **Cobos**, (One's actions are in the human landscape),

- *"The Book of The Community"*, **Mario Rodrigues Cobos** (contains all the basic themes, explanations and notes, including all "The Guided Experiences"),
- *"Self-Liberation"*, **Louis A. Amman**, (A technical manual describing techniques helpful for Self-Awareness).

Themes:

- **The 3 Pathways of Suffering:**
  1: The Past *(what has happened)*,
  2: The Present *(what is happening now, past & future acting in the present)*,
  3: The Future *(fear about what will or might happen)*.

- **The Principles of Valid Action:**
  1: The Principle of Adaptation
  To go against the evolution of things is to go against yourself.

  2: The Principle of Action and Reaction
  When you force something towards an end you produce the contrary.

  3: The Principle of Timely Action
  Do not oppose a great force; retreat until it weakens, then advance with resolution.

  4: The Principle of Proportion
  Things are well when they move together, not in isolation.

  5: The Principle of Contentment
  If day and night, summer and winter are fine with you, you have overcome the contradictions.

  6: The Principle of Pleasure
  If you pursue pleasure, you enchain yourself to suffering. But as long as you do not harm your health, enjoy without inhibition when the opportunity presents itself.

  7: The Principle of Immediate Action
  If you pursue an end you enchain yourself. If everything you do is realized as though it were an end in itself, you liberate yourself.

8: The Principle of Comprehended Action
You will make your conflicts disappear when you understand them in their ultimate roots, not when you want to resolve them.

9: The Principle of Freedom
When you harm others you remain enchained, but if you do not harm anyone you can freely do whatever you want.

10: The Principle of Solidarity
When you treat others as you would have them treat you, you liberate yourself.

11: The Principle of Negating Opposites
It does not matter in which faction events have placed you. What matters is for you to comprehend that you have not chosen any faction.

12: The Principle of Accumulation of Actions
Contradictory and unifying acts accumulate within you. If you repeat your acts of internal unity, nothing can stop you.

- **The Aphorisms:**
  1: "Thoughts produce and attract actions."
  2: "Thoughts with faith produce and attract stronger actions"
  3: "Thoughts repeated with faith produce and attract the maximum strength in one's actions."

- **Levels of Consciousness:**
  There are three levels of *"Consciousness"*.

1: Sleep
Data floods the *"Consciousness"* from one's *"Internal Landscape"* (memories) and internal bodily functions. Very little data comes into the *"Consciousness"* from the external world. There are minimal actions in the external world.

2: Semi-Sleep:
When data floods the *"Consciousness"* from one's *"Internal Landscape"* (memories), internal bodily operations and external triggers but still acting in the world.
This our *"normal"* daily state.
The *"State of Reverie"* (dreaming whilst "awake") and *"Magical/Emotional Consciousness"* occurs in the *"State of Semi-Sleep"*.

In this state responses are mechanical, determined and controlled by behavioural habits.

3: Awake (Consciousness):
The *"Consciousness"* controls and directs one's actions. A state desired to be achieved.
"Intentionality" is the act when the *"Consciousness"* directs operations and actions in the world. The operation of the *"Consciousness"* to operate freely and to direct actions rather than being directed by situations, memories from the past, fears of the future or problems face in the present.
"Intentionality" characterises this state.

- **Theory of Impulses:**

  Objects/Images are charged (positively or negativity) and consequently control the *"Consciousness"*.
  The objective is for the *"Consciousness"* to direct actions not the objects/images.

- **Space of Representation:**
  The screen inside your head where all objects/images are placed and seen.

- **Transference:**
  The moving of charge from an object/image.

- **Transcendence:**
  To no longer fear *"Death"*.
  "He who dies before he dies will NEVER die!"

- **The Light:** the energy within you.
  Inner Peace manifests itself *as "The Light"*!

- **The Force:** the life Force within you.
  Inner Strength manifests itself as *"The Force"*!

- **Reverie Nucleus:** the root of all one's fears.
  Mine was the fear of failure.

- **The Religious Feeling:**
  The feeling of oneness and of a connection with everything.
  It has nothing to do with organised religion.

- **Biotypes:**
  1: Vegetative
  2: Motor
  3: Emotional
  4: Intellectual
  Fixed biological forms/types that one is born with.
  Determined by *"Nature"*.
  Can be modified.

- **Mechanicity/Determinism:**
  Acting without "Intentionality". This is how we act in our daily life. Our actions, behaviours, thoughts and feelings are ALL predetermined beforehand. There is NO freedom of choice. This is just an ILLUSION. Behaviour is purely mechanistic and our behaviour is determined by our past behaviours.

- **Objectification:**

  Turning humans into disposable objects for one's own personal gratification.
  "Do not IMPOSE your Internal Landscape onto others!"

- **Dispossession:**
  The ability to move freely in one's "Internal Landscape".

- **Steps of a Process:**
  1: Differentiation *(separate entities with very little interaction amongst each other)*
  2: Complementation *(interaction amongst separate entities starts taking place and connections start forming)*
  3: Synthesis *(complete unity with a common purpose and goal)*
  This process is now repeated with a new *Differentiation* from the previous *Synthesis*, leading to great and great complexity.

- **Techniques:**
  *Relaxation
  *The Experience of Peace
  *Experience of the Force
  *Guided Experiences

Experience with the Force

Completely relax your body and quiet your mind.

Now, imagine a transparent and luminous sphere. Let it descent towards you until it comes to rest in your heart.

You will notice that the sphere begins to transform into an expanding senstation within your chest.

The sensation of the sphere expands from your chest towards the outside of your body as you breathe more deeply.

You begin to feel new sensations in your hands and the rest of your body.

You will feel undulations and emotions and positive memories will spring forth.

Let the passage of the Force happen freely; this Force give energy your body and your mind.

Let the Force manifest within you. Try to see it's light within your eyes and do not stop it from acting by itself.

Feel the Force and it'd internal brilliance. Let it manifest freely.

Return to the world of daily life strengthened and at peace with yourself. Return to the world of daily life with your hands and forehead luminous.

http://www.silo.net/en/present_transmission/index
http://www.humanistmovement.net/http
s://web.archive.org/web/20080820092355/http://www.ex-silo.org/index.php

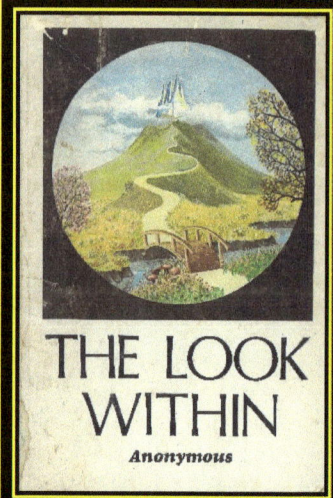

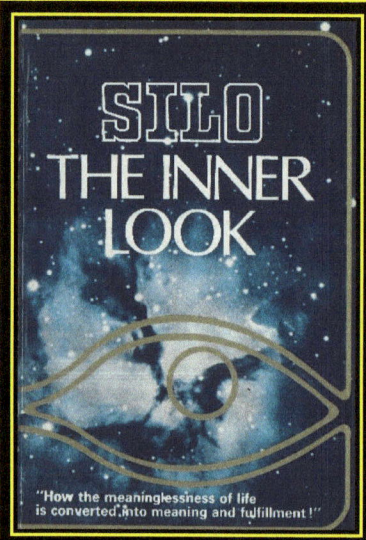

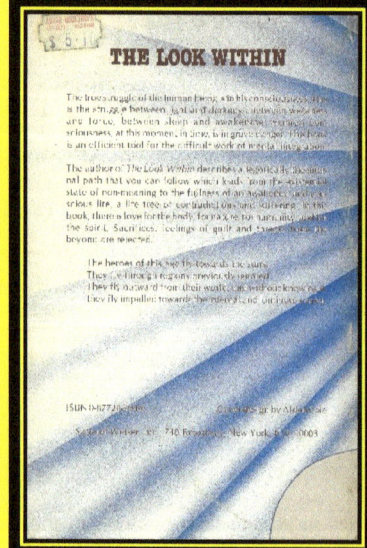
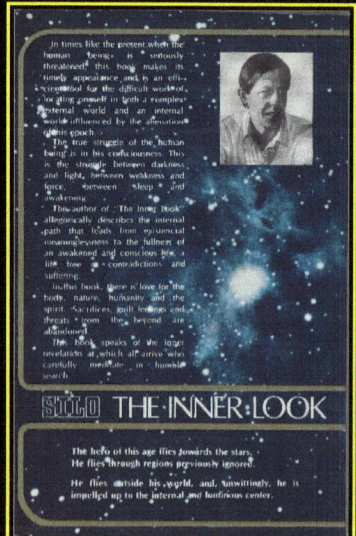

Books written by Mario Rodriguez Cobos (Silo)

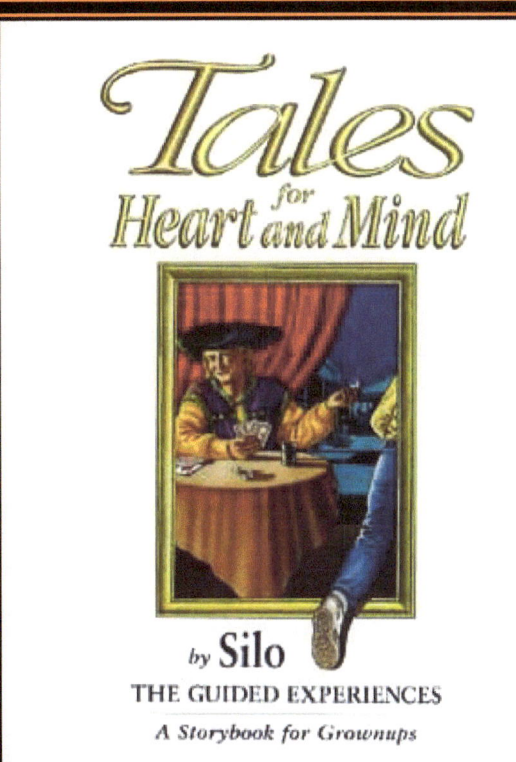
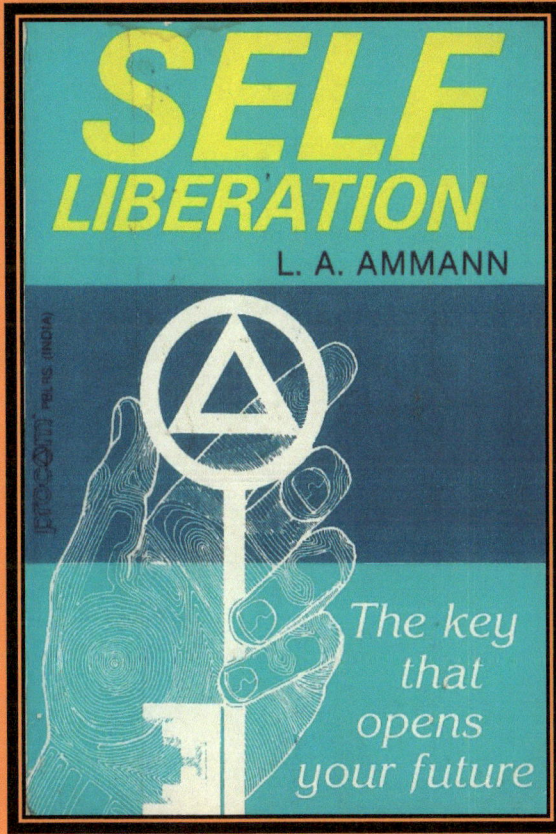

Books used for "Internal Work"

Drawings illustrating the "Principles of Valid Action"

Drawings illustrating themes from "The Internal Landscape"

The Structural Work:

This was about organisation, levels, rules and growth, which a lot of people found hard and difficult to understand or accept, resulting in people not participating actively or leaving altogether.

Although I found it difficult and did not necessarily agree with it, I intellectually understood the need for it, why it existed and why it needed to exist.

The Structure was based on *"Lines"* and *"Levels"*. A member belonged to both.

- **Levels:**
  These were horizontal groups.

  1: Adherent/Member
  2: Active/Active Member
  3: School/Delegate
  4: Order/General Delegate

A member moved up the levels based on the number of members they oriented in their groups.
- Ten *"Active Members"* and you were promoted to the next level of a *"School Member"*.
- Ten *"School Members"* and you were promoted to the next level of an *"Order Member"*.
- Ten *"Order Members"* and you were promoted to the next level of a *"Magister"*.

- **Lines:**
  These were vertical.

A member belonged to a specific individual's *"Line"*. I initially belonged to *"Tito's Line"* through *Nestor* and later on, *Nestor* was moved over to *"Antonio Carvallo's Line"* he became our new Orientor (co-ordinator), who lived in Sri Lanka.

"Lines" were later given symbols of the Greek alphabet. *"Antonio's Line"* was called *"PSI"*.

This information was all in a booklet called *"The Norms of Organisation of the Community for Human Development"*.

- **Theory if Organisation:**
  Differentiated Functions:
  Structural, Support, Administration
  Specialising in:
  Structural: expansion
  Support: Internal work
  Administration: logistics

The biggest impediment for people participating for any long periods of time was the financial commitment. This was especially a problem for young people, students and the unemployed or poor.

The financial commitment was a quarter of the monthly wage in that country. It was collected at the *"Seasonal Assembly"* which happened four times a year; 21st December, 21st March, 21st June & the 21st September.

Here the census also took place, which was the official data and the funds collected was sent back, via the lines determining the number of members at this particular point in time. It was also where any promotions or ceremonies took place. It was also an occasion to share a meal together and have fun, once the formal parts were over.

However, it was at this very point where problems occurred and I believe these problems were system and global. The data collected was not reliable!

Data was faked!

The number of members claimed and the real numbers did not correlate. Even though the funds collected equated to a specific number, those people did not actually exist. The Orientor, in many cases put the funds in and claimed that number of members at their meeting that they attended, which in fact was not true.

This is what, unfortunately, *Nestor* was doing!

So in 1983, it all came to a head for *Nestor*.

Antonio moved to Sydney, Australia in November 1984.

Antonio was Argentinian from Buenos Aires. He was tall and held himself with an air of authority. He was always impeccably dressed and had a casual elegance about him. He claimed that was because of his father's background, being a military man and he himself having been sent to a military school.

I was impressed by him straight away! He seemed very cultured to me!

I liked his style!

In fact, I copied it!

Within a month *Nestor* had imploded and left!

A new chapter had begun!

I saw *Nestor* a few more times, once, late on a Saturday night in Kings Cross, Sydney. He was surrounded by group of girls, sitting in front of a bank. He was still wearing white clothes, although somewhat dishevelled and looking quite "out of it"!

I think he had become a "guru"!

The last time I saw him was in Florence, Italy at the *"First Congress of The International Humanist Party"*. He looked fantastic and seemed to be in good spirits.

A couple of years later I heard that he had been killed in road accident in Santiago, Chile!

I was shocked!

I couldn't believe it!

I was very sad!

I cried!

Tears welled up in my eyes! They rolled down my cheeks, down over my lips down my chin.

I felt that something had been torn from inside me, that I had lost a part of me.

It affected my greatly and I was surprised by that!

I had not really thought that much about him, if at all.
Funny how things affect you!

Nestor

Antonio

"The Don" & Antonio

Vito RADICE

Being a peace-loving, apolitical, curly-headed, simple man, Vito decided to test his patience, endurance and stamina by undertaking the Gorilla (?) training course of Chem. Eng.

Vito is an admirer of fast cars and very slow women. Who would have thought that this quiet, gentle, considerate and conservative boy, would have developed into a rampaging, raging, red-haired, radical.

Trying to realise his ambition to become either a professional wanker or a philosopher he has become a respected member of the community.

Vito's love of the course is matched only by the length of his Italian radish. 'Vital' as he is known to his followers, hopes one day to become high priestess of his community group.

Chapter 4: The (Great) Escape (from the nest)
I gotta get outta of this place!

We Gotta Get Out Of This Place

In this dirty old part of the city
Where the sun refused to shine
People tell me there ain't no use in tryin'

Now my girl, you're so young and pretty
And one thing I know is true
You'll be dead before your time is due, I know

Watch my daddy in bed a-dyin'
Watched his hair been turnin' grey
He's been workin' and slavin' his life away, oh yes I know it

And I've been workin' too, baby (yeah!)
Every night and day (yeah, yeah, yeah, yeah!)

We gotta get out of this place
If it's the last thing we ever do
We gotta get out of this place
'Cause girl, there's a better life for me and you

Now my girl you're so young and pretty
And one thing I know is true, yeah
You'll be dead before your time is due, I know it

Watch my daddy in bed a-dyin'
Watched his hair been turnin' grey, yeah
He's been workin' and slavin' his life away
I know he's been workin' so hard

We gotta get out of this place
If it's the last thing we ever do
We gotta get out of this place
Girl, there's a better life for me and you
Believe me baby
I know it baby
You know it too

Performed by: The Animals
Songwriters: Barry Mann / Cynthia Weil

My father was an angry man!

On 31st August 1983, it was the afternoon and Greg was over. We were in the lounge room having a smoke (tobacco), having a glass of wine, Greg asked for some cheese and bread so I went into the kitchen where my father was sitting at the kitchen table fuming. I knew he was angry but I didn't know what he was angry about! Stupidly, I asked him and he just went ballistic. He blew his top, shouting at the top of his voice, pacing up and down the kitchen floor (he'd gotten up from his chair), frothing at the mouth, beating his hairy chest (he didn't have a shirt on, he was often bare-chested), going completely crazy!

The issue that had triggered this outrageous reaction was my taking cheese and bread to Greg!

How dare I do such a heinous act!

Offer cheese, bread & wine to my friend!

He didn't know him!

He didn't want to know him!

He was a stranger in his house!

He should leave!

"NEVER TRUST the PEOPLE!"

So that evening I decided to escape!

I rang Nestor and Angelika who were living in Summer Hill at the time and asked them if I could stay at their place! They had a spare room off the kitchen. They said yes, so the next morning, I packed as much as I could into my trusty and very reliable, light blue Toyota Corolla, JOM403. It had a four cylinder 1.1 Litre engine (which, for you car enthusiasts will know, is a very small engine)!

What a car that was!

We had so many adventures with that car. It was truly an amazing vehicle. It never broke down, ran on the "smell of an oily rag". I used to put $5 of petrol every week. It was only supposed to carry four passengers, that's including the driver but I'm sure we managed to fit in eight once!
It was stolen and trashed on the 12th December 1989.

But I digress………..

I left that morning, the first day of Spring (1st September) 1983.

I was twenty four years old!

I rang my mother that afternoon to tell her I had left. She had not yet been into my bedroom so she was still unaware. She started to cry and said "Come back, he's not home from work yet, he won't even know!" I told her I could not live there anymore! My time had come to leave and that I was sorry that I was hurting her but it was something that I had to do! She cried even more! So, I told her that I loved her and that would always love her, said goodbye and hung up the phone!

My brother and father found me in three days!

Apparently, I had left my little address book with my friends' names in it, so they rang them all asking if they knew where I was. Some of their replies to leaving were very funny, "Well, about time he left home!", "Congratulations!", "No, I didn't know but I'll tell him that you're looking for him, if I see him!", "Fantastic", "I'm sure he'd tell you if he wanted you to know where he was!", "He should've left a long time ago, if you ask me!" and "How old is he again?".

It was 1:00pm on the Sunday afternoon when there was a knock on the front door. Angelika went to see who it was. I was in my small room out the back. She came to call me and I could see that she looked very nervous, I asked what was wrong and she told me that there were two men at the front door, one of them said that he was my brother and that he wanted to talk to me.

I walked out through the kitchen, where Nestor was seated at the kitchen table, along the corridor which led to the lounge room in to the hallway corridor where I could see my brother standing outside the front door entrance, flanked by his father-in-law, Michaele. I walked past the two bedrooms and reached the front entrance and greeted my brother and Michaele.

All this time, as I was making my way to the front door, I was slightly nervous and anxious about what I was about to face and how to respond and handle it.

My brother told me that our father was in the Valiant and that he wanted to see me and talk to me. I walked out after them and followed them to where they had parked the car. My father was sitting in the backseat. I opened the front door and sat in the front seat. He was crying.

I asked him why was he crying? He said, *"Come home, I forgive you!"* I told him that there was nothing to forgive but I could not go home! He kept on crying and then he said *"Forgive me if I've done anything wrong"*. I told him that I forgave him. That I loved him but I could not go home with him. Still crying he said *"Even Jesus forgave those that wronged him"*. I repeated myself that I could no longer live with him and that it was time for me to leave. He said that I had a heart of stone. Upon which I said goodbye to him, opened the car door said goodbye to my brother and Michaele, who been standing a little distance away under the shade of a shop awning and went back to my new home.

My father was still crying.

I did not see or speak to him for the next six months!

"The Don"

Chapter 5: The Humanist Party: Humanise the Earth

Rehumanise Yourself

He goes out at night with his big boots on
None of his friends know right from wrong
They kick a boy to death 'cause he don't belong
You've got to humanize yourself

A policeman put on his uniform
He'd like to have a gun just to keep him warm
Because violence here is a social norm
You've got to humanize yourself

Re-humanize yourself

I work all day at the factory
I'm building a machine that's not for me
There must be a reason that I can't see
You've got to humanize yourself

Billy's joined the National Front
He always was a little runt
He's got his hand in the air with the other cunts
You've got to humanize yourself

Re-humanize yourself

I work all day at the factory
I'm building a machine that's not for me
There must be a reason that I can't see
You've got to humanize yourself

A policeman put on his uniform
He'd like to have a gun just to keep him warm
Because violence here is a social norm
You've got to humanize yourself

Re-humanize yourself

Performed by" The Police
Songwriters: Gordon Sumner / Stewart Copeland

In the *"Council Meeting of General Co-ordinators"* (the highest level in the organisation chaired by *Cobos*) of the 21st June 1983, it was decided that *"The Community"* would launch a political party to be called *"The Humanist Party"*.

The *"The Community"* would cease to exist!

This news was delivered to everyone by *Nestor*.

We were all SHOCKED!

A political party?

What did we know about politics?

The answer was a simple one: You learn by doing!

The reason: destructive events in the world were accelerating at a dangerous rate and that the only effective response to this time of great crisis was a political one.

We had to get our people in the political system and get our hands on the levers of power because those in power were destroying the planet!

How prophetic was that!

"The Humanist Party of Australia" was launched on Sunday 2nd August 1983 at the University of Technology (then, the Institute of Technology), Sydney.

The symbol of *"The Humanist Party"* was the **"Mobius Loop"**!

"The Mobius Loop", is an old geometric design (sometimes referred to as **"Sacred Geometry"**) which represents the interconnection between the inside of an entity and its outside.

They are but one and the same.

There is no distinction.

No separation.

No conflict.

No imbalance.

Perfect equilibrium.

Perfect balance.

Perfect harmony.

I was the President and spokesperson of the party (unanimously elected).

This was a scary proposition for me but I accepted the challenge with enthusiasm, good will and a lot of bravado.

It was a steep learning curve for me. I knew very little of politics so I had to learn fast.

And I did!

It was a new adventure for me and everyone involved and what an adventure it would become!

Straight away our weekly meetings became about political discussions and planning strategies and activities.

We had to make new materials, banners, leaflets, pamphlets, booklets, newsletters and newspapers.

Get involved in political activities and get members to join the new party.

To do this we went to the streets, stopped people, talked to them and asked them if they were interested and if they were, to join the *"Humanist Party"*!

"The Community" was DEAD!

"Internal work" was set aside!

Most of my friends who I had joined with and had introduced me to *"The Community"* left!

I was the last man standing!

It was a very steep learning curve. We had to write a constitution, policies, decide on political agenda, strategies and tactics. No easy task for political novices!

But we were committed and believed in what we were doing.

We managed to get *"The Humanist Party"* office in the old *Peggy Lee Building*, opposite Hyde Park, in front of Museum Station on Elizabeth Street, Sydney.

The rent was cheap and the location was to die for. Directly opposite Hyde Park on Elizabeth, just around the corner from Liverpool Street, Sydney!

The building was populated by all manner of people, arty, prostitutes, political parties, musicians, and other desperadoes and fringe dwellers!

What a *"multi-cultural"* community we were!

What a great location!

We had two rooms in this ramshackle of an old building. It even had one of those old style open-caged lifts.

It was truly a FANTASTIC place.

This was our centre of operations. One room (the larger one) on the third floor. was used for meetings and the second (smaller), was used for the production of materials, banners placards, newsletters, leaflets and as a general storage space.

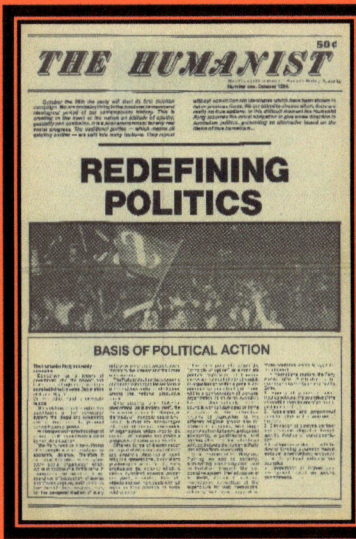

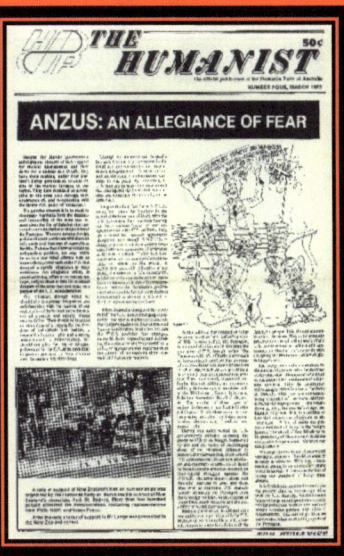

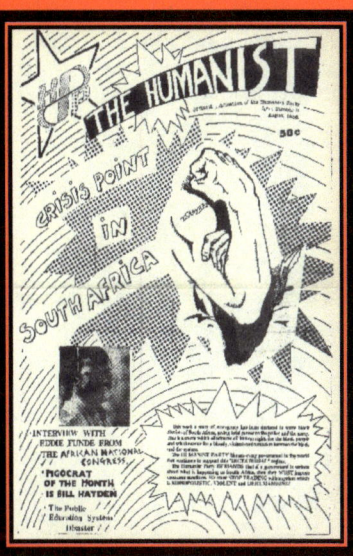

"The Humanist": the official paper of the Humanist Party of Australia

Chapter 6: The Campaign: Petition for a Referendum to Close Pine Gap 1985-1986

US Forces

US Forces give the nod, it's a setback for your country
Bombs and trenches all in rows, bombs and threats still ask for more
Divided world the CIA, who controls the issue
You leave us with no time to talk, you can write your assessment

Sing me songs of no denying, seems to me too many trying
Waiting for the next big thing
Will you know it when you see it, high risk children dogs of war
Now market movements call the shots, business deals in parking lots
Waiting for the meat of tomorrow

Sing me songs

Everyone is too stoned to start emission
People too scared to go to prison
We're unable to make decision
Political party line don't cross that floor
Lt. Ron Hubbard can't save your life
Superboy takes a plutonium wife
In the shadow of Ban The Bomb we live

Performed by: Midnight Oil
Songwriters: James Moginie/Martin Rotsey/Peter Garrett/Peter Gifford/Robert Hirst

The late 1980s were turbulent political times globally.

Ronald Reagan (former governor of California and b-grade movie actor was US president and Mikhail Gorbachev was president of the Soviet Union (USSR).

The biggest nuclear power plant accident in the history had occurred in Chernobyl, Ukraine in 1986 killing and injuring hundreds of thousands of people (an exact number has never been possible to determine), contaminating most of Europe and establishing a thirty kilometre radius exclusion zone for the next one thousand years.

The world was in a state of great upheaval and flux.

Nuclear disarmament was on top of the agenda for a lot of people and there were enormous rallies worldwide demanding action!

Australia was no different!

It was in this political environment that the lease for the US Military Defence installation in the centre of Australia was up for renewal.

The installation is called *"Pine Gap"*, a joint US-Australian run facility.
It gathers intelligence from around the world via satellites orbiting the planet, sending this information directly to The Pentagon.

This makes it an extremely sensitive facility and a first strike target, in the event of a nuclear confrontation.

Not a good situation for Australia to be in, I would have thought!

We took on the challenge!

We sought a referendum for people to decide whether the lease on "Pine Gap" should be renewed or not.

We thought that people should have a say on these vital decisions that directly affected their very existence!

Over a nine month period from June 1985 to March 1986 we ran an intensive campaign collecting for a petition asking the government to have a referendum on this issue.

We campaigned almost every day, going out on the streets, talking to people and collecting signatures.

We went all over Sydney, put up banners, a card table with information and the petition for people to sign.

We also brought the "big gun", every protester's main tool of the trade, the *"megaphone"*!

This was quite daunting and scary at first. It takes a lot of guts to use one and it's NOT for everyone!

There are many ways to approach using a *"megaphone"* but it is not an easy instrument to use effectively!

There are those who shout into the mouthpiece, very emotional and expressing one's passion for their cause BUT not very effective because it is a very aggressive method. The message is physically distorted because the mouthpiece cannot cope with the barrage of vibrations and spit coming out of one's mouth, resulting in complete distortion, noise and abrasiveness for the poor passerby. A very uncomfortable and sometimes painful experience. All a person walking past wants to do, is get as far away from there as quickly as possible.

Walk as fast as you can, don't make eye-contact!

A real TURNOFF!

Then there is the person who has a very high pitched, shrilly voice, again very painful for the poor passerby.

Finally, there is the very softly spoken, almost whispering voice which is so unobtrusive, it negates the purpose of using the *"megaphone"* in the first place. One might as well be a statue. Completely ineffective.

My approach was to use a very modulated voice and allowing the *"megaphone"* to the work for me. I did not have the volume turned up to maximum, which instantly causes that annoying feedback distortion common to most *"megaphone"* users but is exactly the first thing most users do, in the mistaken belief that it is all about VOLUME! The need to be heard! On the contrary, the most important thing is to be UNDERSTOOD!

I used a low timbre voice, spoke slowly and clearly. I NEVER shouted!

People don't like being shouted at!

I tried to engage people rather than harangue them!

We managed to collect over 60,000 signatures!

An amazing accomplishment by such a small party!

We handed the petition to The Nuclear Disarmament Party Senator, Robert Woods who tabled it in Parliament.

Robert Woods was elected as a NSW senator in the 1987 Federal election. However, the High Court declared his election was invalid as he was not an Australian citizen at the time. He was not entitled to be nominated for election as a senator and therefore had never been validly elected. He was replaced by *Irene Dunn*, second on the ballot ticket.

It was our most successful campaign!

I was very proud of what we were able to achieve!

I still am!

Poster for the "Close Pine Gap Rally", designed by Anna Nummarun

Pine Gap — The facts

Australia's most controversial US controlled military base is an extensive installation. Its presence in Australia has caused more heated debate than any other overseas interest in this country, yet the Hawke government still refrains from publicising the FACTS. Information about the base must be sought out through intensive research — limiting awareness about Pine Gap to those annoyed by an un-democratic attitude towards society. The average Australian therefore receives no information. Approximately 15 percent of Australians do not even know the US has installations in this country.

Pine Gap is situated 50 kilometers North-West of Alice Springs in the Northern Territory. The operational area of the Base (code named MERINO) covers over one square kilometre. A sixteen square kilometre security zone surrounds the operations centre. A check point is situated on the road from Alice Springs and a double fencing system forms the perimiter of the security zone. The fence is patrolled by armed security guards 24 hours a day. The road is one of the few bitumen carriage ways in the south of the Northern Territory.

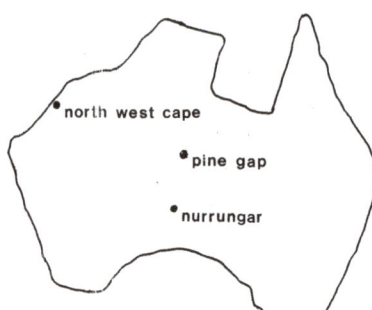

Planes may not fly within a radius of 4km from Pine Gap. Visitors may not enter the properties surrounding the security zone. Pine Gap is supposed to be staffed by equal numbers of Australians and Americans, but this is not so. The only Australians are cleaners, cooks, and some basic maintenance staff. All positions of any importance are held by American Government staff — Australians are the servants.

Much evidence has been accumulated pointing towards the possibility of a nuclear power station at Pine Gap. The base uses a massive quantity of water and large quantities of water are needed for the cooling of a reactor. This water to a large degree, is not recyclable — it is passed off as steam. The official claim is that six 1500 horsepower diesel generators power the base — but diesel motors do not require anywhere near the huge quantities of water used by Pine Gap. Much more evidence exists for the presence of a reactor at Pine Gap.

The "Domes" that are the predominant feature of the Gap are weather protectors for the antennae that form the communications links on just about every radio frequency. Pine Gap is the main communications link for the US submarine fleet.

Pine Gap has direct communications link with the Clarke base in the Phillipines. Most recently, Pine Gap has taken on the function of control centre for the Omega spy-satellite system over the eastern half of the USSR. The Omega satelite is the core of the US early warning defence system — this factor alone makes Pine Gap a FIRST STRIKE NUCLEAR TARGET. In the event of a USA-USSR relations breakdown the first targets are the early warning systems — the intelligence systems. We are threatened by a foreign interest in this country without the consent of Australians through democratic means; we as Australians are being threatened by a so-called allie.

Pine Gap contains an extensive network of underground corridors and rooms. The main computer room covers an area of over 200 square metres and is still being extended. The entire base is completely self-contained and is obviously intended as shelter from a war-ravaged plant.

Only top-ranking CIA personnel man the computer room. All information received by the base that could possibly be of use to the Australian military is first screened by the CIA. We get to know what the CIA would like us to know.

And what has Pine Gap cost? Besides the obvious and severe threat it poses to every Australian, it has been stated that it would required over USA $1.5 billion to replace the installation. How much of this bill has the Australian government contributed? How much is the Hawke government paying to help threaten its citizens?

US Military Bases within Australia—are they a necessity or do they make us a target?
This is the question that many Australians have debated over, yet still no concrete policy in relation to the bases has evolved within the present Labor government. Hawke takes the stand of 'mutual benefit', yet the majority of his cabinet remains completely undecided. The left wing of the Labor party—what remains of it—will not take a firm stand against the bases as it continually finds itself burdened with the confusing dilectic support by the right wing of the Labor movement. The right maintains its anti-democratic policies by remaining in secret collaboration with the White House and so no decision is ever actually made in relation to US involvement in Australian affairs.

Lets look at some of the history of the major installation controlled by the US on Australian soil—Pine Gap. This is one of over thirty bases in Australia used by the US for their own defense purposes.

Pine Gap was established under an agreement with the US on the 9th of December, 1966. The co-operating US agency listed was the Defense Advanced Research Projects Agency. This was later amended on the 19th of December, 1977 to simply the US Department Of Defense. Three US intelligence organisations have been documented as being involved, namely The National Reconnaisance Office (NRO), The National Security Agency (NRA) and the now well-publicised CIA.

Pine Gap officially became operational in 1970 and is functionally known as The US-Australian Joint Defense Space Reserch Facility. Pine Gap is an extensive installation. It is completely self-contained and no-one can enter without the appropriate clearance within a radius of four kilometers. Planes cannot fly over an extensive prohibited area.

The first chief of this facility was CIA officer Richard Lee Stallings.

The agreement for the establishment of Pine Gap was signed in 1970 by the then Minister for External Affairs, Mr Paul Hasluck. It was initially to remain in force for ten years, until the 9th of December, 1976 and thereafter until termination but it was extended for a further ten years by the 'Exchange of notes' on the 19th of October 1977, **without opposition**.

After the 19th of October, 1986 either government can request termination of the lease with one years notice.

The decision to establish Pine Gap, and the decision to extend the lease were both made in a cloak of secrecy, without the consultation of the Australian public.

It is documented fact that Pine Gap has been from the beginning a CIA installation. All the Chiefs of the Facility have been CIA officers, with The Department Of Defense operating in name as a cover.

The principal function that the "Gap" serves is one of communications. It contains a number of high-frequency antennae and collectors and is in direct communication with the Clark US military base in the Philippines. It is a key link in the US Defense Early warning communications network.

So, these are its claimed and more obvious functions. But how much occurs within the confines of Pine Gap that is unknown to the Australian public? Is this bases' functions totally directed towards defense? Within some of the current military strategies, it is almost impossible to determine the fine line between Defense and Offense, so how can we justify its presence in this country without compromise?

The Labour Government will not disclose the true functions of Pine Gap—it will not even take the viewpoint of speculation. Most of the functions made public have come from ex-CIA members, infiltrators and careful observation of external connections.

In reality, it is only the "hard right" of the Labor party, led by Bob Hawke that does not challenge the presence of Pine Gap. Included on the list of members of parliament that have spoken out against the Gap are Joan Coxsedge, Joe Camilleri, and most significantly the Minister for Defense Mr Beazley and the Minister for Foreign Affairs, John Howard.

In early 1984 the Left Wing of the Labour Party put forward motions for the winding down of North West Cape, Pine Gap and Nurrungar. The proposals were defeated by a vote of 55 to 43.

So what is holding the Bases in Australia?

All conclusions (and much concrete evidence) points to the fact that the chief decision makers of the Hawke government are in liasion with the policies of the White House and Pentagon. The Hawke Government has been effectively "bought out"—It is not acting in consideration of the Australian Public.

This is a gross misuse of the faith of the Australian public and an inexcusable abuse of Human rights.

The Bases will stay until sufficient pressure is supplied by Australian people who are interested in their democratic rights. □

The Humanist page 2

Chapter 7:   The Elections 1984-1988

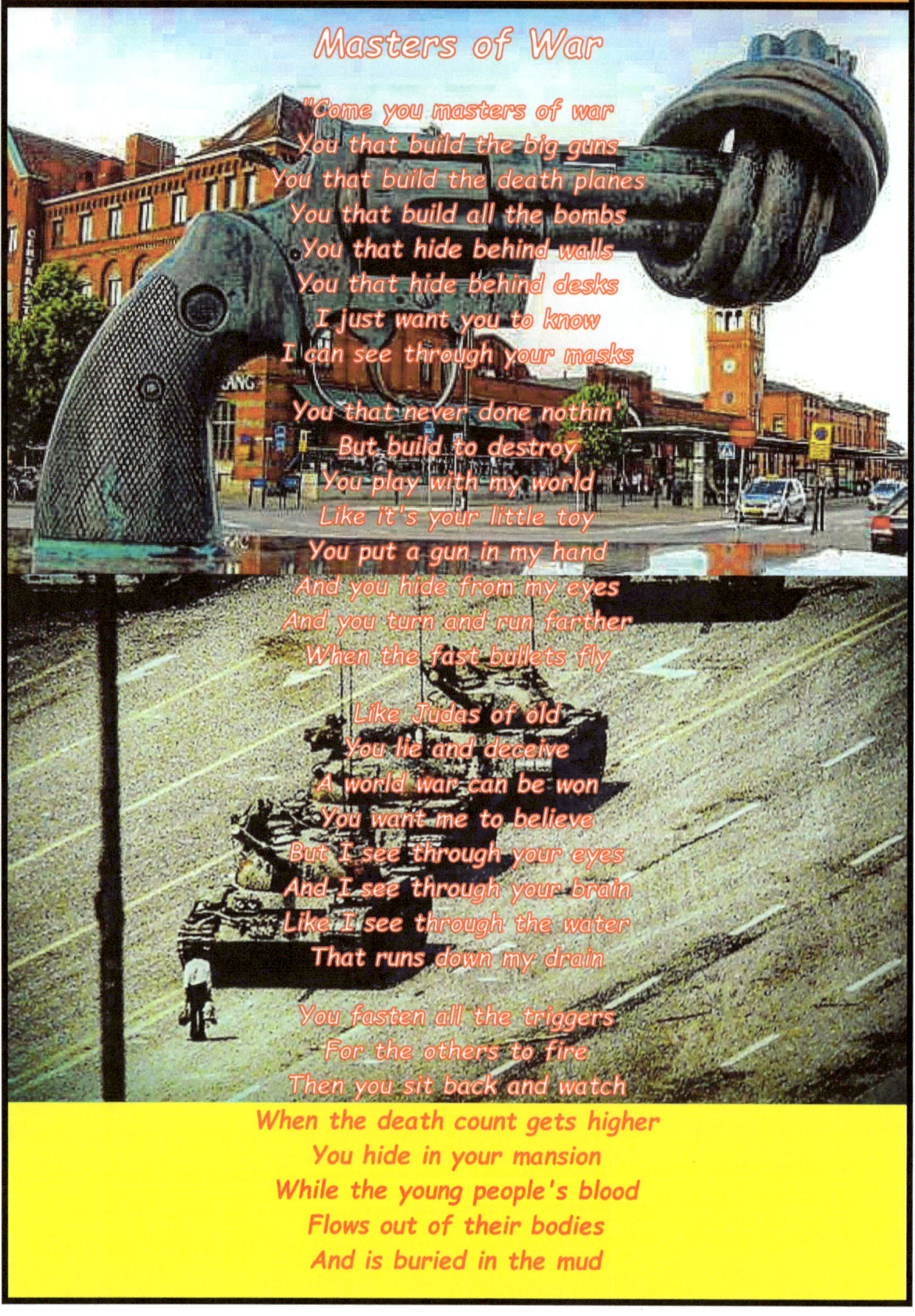

Masters of War

"Come you masters of war
You that build the big guns
You that build the death planes
You that build all the bombs
You that hide behind walls
You that hide behind desks
I just want you to know
I can see through your masks

You that never done nothin'
But build to destroy
You play with my world
Like it's your little toy
You put a gun in my hand
And you hide from my eyes
And you turn and run farther
When the fast bullets fly

Like Judas of old
You lie and deceive
A world war can be won
You want me to believe
But I see through your eyes
And I see through your brain
Like I see through the water
That runs down my drain

You fasten all the triggers
For the others to fire
Then you sit back and watch
When the death count gets higher
You hide in your mansion
While the young people's blood
Flows out of their bodies
And is buried in the mud

You've thrown the worst fear
That can ever be hurled
Fear to bring children
Into the world
For threatening my baby
Unborn and unnamed
You ain't worth the blood
That runs in your veins

How much do I know
To talk out of turn
You might say that I'm young
You might say I'm unlearned
But there's one thing I know
Though I'm younger than you
That even Jesus would never
Forgive what you do

Let me ask you one question
Is your money that good?
Will it buy you forgiveness
Do you think that it could?
I think you will find
When your death takes its toll
All the money you made
Will never buy back your soul

And I hope that you die
And your death will come soon
I'll follow your casket
By the pale afternoon
And I'll watch while you're lowered
Down to your deathbed
And I'll stand over your grave
'Til I'm sure that you're dead."

Songwriter: Bob Dylan

1984:
Federal Elections: NSW Senate
Candidate: Vito Radice
1st December, 1984

Our first real test was contesting the 1984 Federal Election.

The 1984 Australian federal election was held on 1st December 1984. The election was held eighteen months ahead of time, partly to bring the elections for the House of Representatives and Senate back into line following the double dissolution election of 1983.

We decided to field a candidate for the NSW lower house seat of *"Sydney"*!

Guess who the candidate was?

Yep! You guessed it!

Me!

This is what happens when you start something. You decide what to do!

Why?

Out of pure necessity!

There is no one else to do it if you don't!

I was twenty five years old!

It gets much more complicated when more people are involved!

The *"Sydney"* electorate covered the inner city that included Newtown, Glebe, Marrickville and the city itself. It was a *"Labor Party"* held seat at the time. The sitting member was *"Peter Baldwin"*.

In hindsight this was probably a mistake. It would probably have been more effective and efficient if we'd contested the NSW Senate, because then electors from all over the state could have been able to vote for us, not just those living in the *"Sydney"* electorate.

A couple of things were against us from the very start:

- Small, unknown party
- Unknown candidate
- Limited funds and resources such as people to help
- Not about to use our logo on the ballot paper

- No media coverage

Not having the *HP* logo on the ballot paper was a huge disadvantage because people could not find us and I was a complete nobody!

To get the logo of a political party onto the ballot paper, the party is required to have a minimum of five hundred registered members or already be a sitting member of parliament.

Getting five hundred registered members, for a new party just starting out is not that easy.

It is no mean feat and quite an obstacle to jump over!

It is very, very difficult.

Especially, when people are apathetic and disillusioned with politicians and politics in general.

Nevertheless, we ran fearless campaign it was a fantastic experience for me.

Our campaign strategy was very simple: go out on the streets every day, stop and talk to people. At night we would go out and plaster walls with posters. My sexy, handsome face was everywhere. Especially in the Devonshire Street tunnel which we plastered both sides of the tunnel from end to end.

No one could miss me!

For glue we would use the, every revolutionaries' tools of the trade: a bucket, a brush, flour and water.

The perfect glue!

Very cheap!

Sometimes we would use sticky tape, to put posters around telegraph poles but this was more expensive.

The incumbent *"Labor Party"* led by *Prime Minister Bob Hawke* defeated the opposition *"Liberal–National Party"* coalition, led *by Andrew Peacock*.

1984 Federal Election poster #1

1984 Federal Election poster #2

					Aileen Beaver (CPA)
Sydney	Labor	Peter Baldwin	James Harker-Mortlock (Lib)	Michael Walsh	Daphne Gollan (Ind)
					Noel Hazard (Ind)
					Vito Radice (Ind)

1984 Australian federal election: Sydney

Party	Candidate	Votes	%	±
Labor	Peter Baldwin	32,412	57.2	-7.0
Liberal	James Harker-Mortlock	12,847	22.7	+1.2
Democrats	Michael Walsh	4,600	8.1	+1.0
Independent	Daphne Gollan	3,118	5.5	+5.5
Independent	Vito Radice	2,219	3.9	+3.9
Communist	Aileen Beaver	1,213	2.1	-1.3
Independent	Noel Hazard	290	0.5	+0.5
Total formal votes		56,699	89.6	
Informal votes		6,601	10.4	
Turnout		63,300	90.2	

1987:
NSW State By-Election: Seat of Bankstown
Candidate: Scott Wilkie
31st January, 1987

Federal Elections: The Senate
Candidates: Ruth Philips, Walter Brun
19th March, 1987

Democrats	1. Paul McLean **(elected 3)** 2. Jenny Macleod 3. Richard Jones 4. Gary Chestnut	290,049	9.1	-0.6
Call to Australia	1. Elaine Nile 2. Kevin Hume	107,859	3.4	-0.2
Nuclear Disarmament	1. Robert Wood **(elected 12)** 2. Irina Dunn	48,998	1.5	-8.2
Greens	1. Ian Cohen 2. Daphne Gollan	32,513	1.0	+1.0
Group A	1. Ruth Phillips 2. Walter Brun	30,504	0.9	+0.9

- **Local Council Elections: Marrickville Council**
Candidates: Vito Radice, Scott Wilkie, Mariclaire Pringle
26th September, 1987

SHAKE, RATTLE AND OPEN

MARRICKVILLE COUNCIL ELECTION
26th September, 1987

VOTE 1 Radice, 2 Wilkie, 3 Pringle for NEWINGTON

HUMANIST PARTY

VOTE FOR THE 'OPEN COUNCIL' TEAM IN NEWINGTON

Number the candidates as shown below.

GROUP A	GROUP B	GROUP C	GROUP D	GROUP E
☐ Nicholls,	☑ 4 Walsh,	☑ 1 RADICE	☐ Elvy,	☑ 7 Gray,
☐ Cotter,	☑ 5 Pritchard-Jones,	☑ 2 WILKIE	☐ Tierney,	☑ 8 Muggleton,
☐ Appleton,	☑ 6 Tihic,	☑ 3 PRINGLE	☐ Hicks,	
☐ Rule,			☐ Madirrazza,	

HUMANIST PARTY

IT'S TIME TO SHAKE UP MARRICKVILLE COUNCIL

REMEMBER COUNCIL ELECTIONS 26th SEPT

COUNCILLORS NEED TO BE ACCOUNTABLE FOR THEIR POLITICAL ACTIONS
The Humanist Party wants to 'open up' Marrickville Council and make it accessible and accountable to all residents.

A NEW STYLE
The Humanist Party intends to introduce a new style in the way that council is run and decisions are made.
It is committed to actively promote and consult residents on every major issue and decision to be made. It will always place residents' needs and concerns ABOVE commercial interests.
It will introduce the method of DIRECT DEMOCRACY, in which the Council has the function of IMPLEMENTING the decisions made by the residents, NOT making decisions.
Vote for the new OPEN STYLE of council.
VOTE 1 HUMANIST PARTY for an OPEN COUNCIL team for **NEWINGTON WARD** in Marrickville Council.

- 1 **Vito Radice**
- 2 **Scott Wilkie**
- 3 **Mariclaire Pringle**

THE HUMANIST TEAM'S POLICIES

POLITICAL ACCOUNTABILITY
It is our primary objective to 'open up' Marrickville Council and for this reason we will adhere to the following policies:
- To make the council accessible to all residents of the municipality.
- To divide the wards up into smaller units (precincts), so that the council is decentralised and the needs of smaller areas catered for.
- No decision will be made about a specific issue unless approved by the residents of that precinct.
- To hold referendums on important issues, so that decisions are made by all residents.
- Proposes that the Mayor, in future council elections, will be elected democratically by the community — not by the Aldermen as is presently the case. This reform is practiced in Canterbury and North Sydney Councils.
- All Aldermen will be obliged to adhere to their pre-election policies. Election of our team will mean an end to underhanded council dealings and 'ripoffs'.

- Information will be made available to residents so that they are kept informed about issues. For this purpose, a monthly 'bulletin' will be produced by the council and distributed free to every household in the community. The bulletin will also allow residents and community groups to have their say and will be an informative newspaper style publication.

COMMUNITY SERVICES
As our interest is in the community, the type and quality of the services that we provide for the use and benefit of every resident is a priority.
It is the responsibility of the whole community to look after, help and support those that are disadvantaged, disabled or just cannot cope with the pressures of our accelerating society.
Marrickville Municipality is made up of residents from many different nations, and they face the difficulties that living in a new country brings.
As a community, it is our responsibility to help them integrate and create better lives for themselves and their families.
The Humanist Party proposes to redirect and reallocate funds to develop more and better community services. These will include:
- Improving the facilities of Marrickville Library.
- Employing more community, social, migrant and youth workers.
- Establishing a Marrickville community radio station.
- Establishing a Marrickville Multicultural Centre.
- Improving and increasing childcare facilities, so that they are cheap and freely available to everyone, especially single parent and low income families.
- Supporting and developing youth initiatives, including job creation projects.
- Supporting and developing activities for pensioners and senior citizens.

URBAN PLANNING
Greater thought and planning needs to be carried out to make sure that the natural environment is not replaced by more buildings, roads, concrete, etc.
The Humanist Party envisages an 'integrated approach' to urban planning — one in which human beings and the natural environment are equally considered.
The Humanist Party proposes the following:
- Make sure that any changes to traffic flow or redevelopment of an area are done with the consultation of all the residents involved.
- Oppose destruction of the environment purely for commercial gain.
- Make sure all existing green areas are maintained and establishing 'greening' projects.
- Oppose the construction of the F5 freeway and the Very Fast Train (V.F.T.).
- Clean up Cooks River and the preservation of Wolli Creek.
- Improvement of general cleaning services such as street cleaning and garbage removal.
- Encourage the development of a more efficient and cheaper public transport system.
- Develop heritage projects.

SHAKE, RATTLE & OPEN MARRICKVILLE COUNCIL
VOTE 1 Radice, 2 Wilkie, 3 Pringle
For NEWINGTON WARD on SEPT. 26th.
HUMANIST PARTY

1988:
NSW State Elections: Legislative Council
Candidates: Vito Radice, Noel Whitaker
19th March, 1988

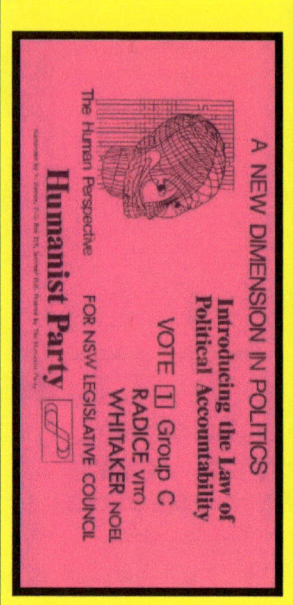

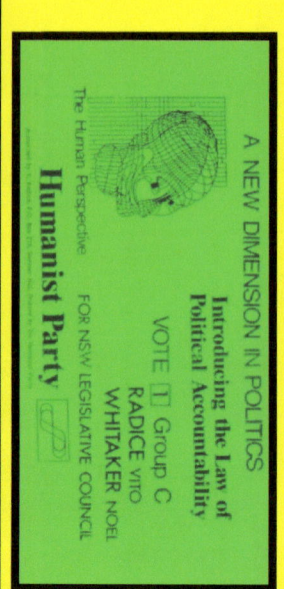
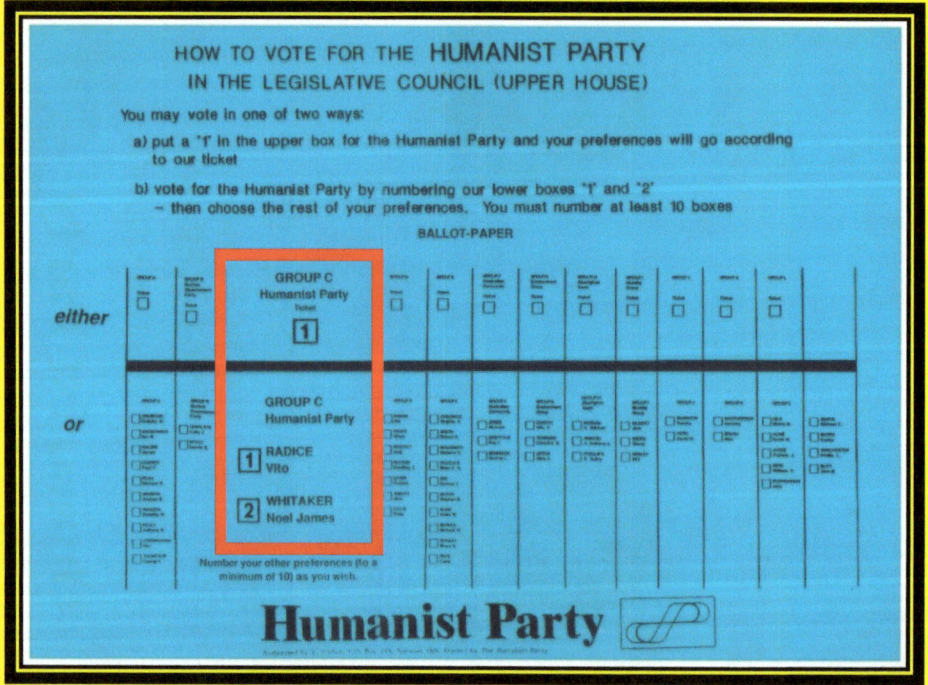

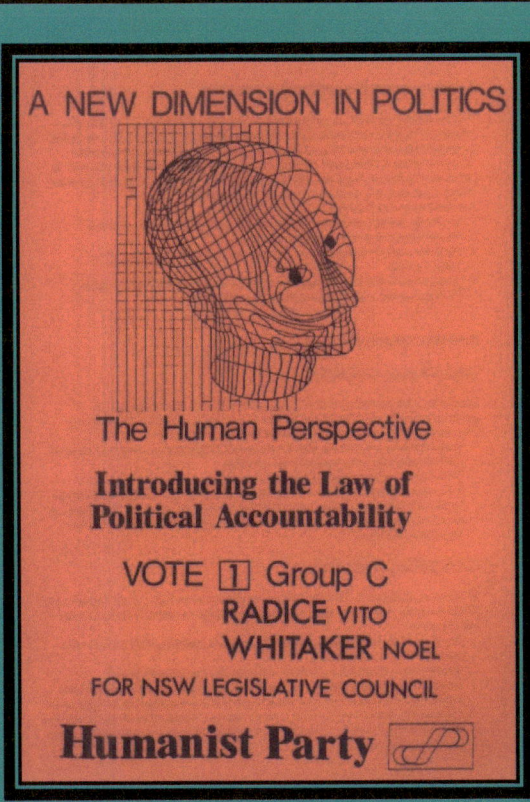

CANDIDATE'S AGREEMENT
(A contract between the Humanist Party and the Candidate)

I, Vito Radice, of 32 Parramatta Rd., Summer Hill

hereby agree to be the candidate for the Humanist Party in the forthcoming parliamentary elections for NSW, fully aware of the nature of the position and its obligations. The conditions of this contract are:

1) I have freely decided to be a Candidate.

2) I am in full agreement with the aims, objectives policies and platforms of the Humanist Party.

3) I am answerable to the Humanist Party and will represent it and no other party.

4) If I am elected and decide to resign from the Humanist Party, I must also resign from my elected position and allow another person, nominated by the Humanist Party, to replace me.

5) If elected, I agree to accept two-thirds of my salary and put the remaining one-third into a party fund to be used for community-based projects.

Signature of Candidate: V. Radice

Signature of witness: John Arnold J.P.

Name and address of witness: 503 Lyons Rd. West, Five Dock 2046

Date: 29·2·88

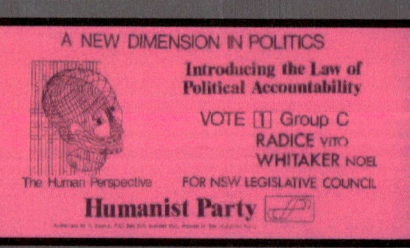

 humanist party

NEWS RELEASE

P.O. BOX 219
SUMMER HILL 2130
799-4601

THE HUMANIST PARTY'S CANDIDATES AGREEMENT

When the public vote for a candidate in the forthcoming elections, they are also voting in support of the philosophies and policies of the party the candidate represents. They could reasonably expect the candidates to forward these policies in parliament.

However, in the current political system there is nothing that binds an elected candidate to the platform on which she/he was elected. A prime example of this occurred after the 1983 Queensland elections, when two Liberals (Lane and Austin) defected to the National Party, betraying their constituents but retaining their ministries.

Furthermore, there is often considerable discrepancies between party policy, as decided by the full membership of the party, and its application by the representatives of the party in parliament. The bitter infighting in the Hawke government over the sale of uranium is a good illustration of this.

The Humanist Party believes that these misuses of representative democracy should not be allowed to arise. We are leading by example, by asking our candidates to sign an agreement binding them to the party and its policies. The conditions of this contract are:

1) I have freely decided to be a candidate.

2) I am in full agreement with the aims, objectives, policies and platforms of the Humanist Party.

3) I am answerable to the Humanist Party and will represent it and no other party.

4) If I am elected and decide to resign from the Humanist Party, I must also resign from my elected position and allow another person, nominated by the Humanist Party, to replace me.

5) If elected, I agree to accept two-thirds of my salary and put the remaining one-third into a party fund to be used for community-based projects.

This stance goes hand in hand with our philosophy of political accountability, which would ensure that parties do not change their policies after an election (see previous press release).

VOTE [1] GROUP "C": RADICE and WHITAKER for the NSW LEGISLATIVE COUNCIL

 humanist party

NEWS RELEASE

P.O. BOX Q299
QUEEN VICTORIA BUILDING
SYDNEY 2001
799-4601

LAW OF POLITICAL ACCOUNTABILTY

Elections are a time when parties present superficially attractive policies with no detail as to how and when they will be implemented. Very few of these promises are carried out after the election during the 4 years when the politicians are not answerable to the people.

The voting public should be able to at any time withdraw their support for a government that is not fulfilling the platform on which it was elected.

The Humanist Party proposes the introduction of a law of political accountability.

1) Party platforms and policies (election promises) should contain detailed information on objectives and methods of implementation and a time schedule for this.

2) These policies will be legally binding documents.

3) If an elected party does not carry out a promised policy in the specified time it will have broken it's contract and will face a new election. At this election.the party can explain the reasons for the breach of contract and the electorate will judge the validity of these.

4) Referendums should be held on major issues so that the whole population can participate in the decision making process. The Humanist Party will introduce people initiated referendums (plebicites), where more than 10% of the voting population petitions parliament. This process will also act as a popular veto on any aspect of the governmental system.

5) Parliament will be televised. This will increase public awareness and participation in the political process and help overcome problems of media manipulation.

6) Candidates are elected on the strength of their party's policies rather than personalities and have a duty to represent these policies in parliament, remaining answerable to their party. The Humanist Party will require it's candidates to sign a contract outlining their commitment to the party.

7) We believe that politicians are overpaid and that recent calls for substantial wage rises are not in line with the government's "policy" of wage restraint. Any Humanist Party candidate that is elected will only accept 2/3 of their salary, the remaining 1/3 will be put into a party fund to finance community based projects.

This policy of political accountability is subject to further discussion and development and we invite comment.

VOTE RADICE and WHITAKER for the NSW LEGISLATIVE COUNCIL

At the recent State election, about 10 000 people gave their No. 1 vote in the Upper House to the Humanist Party - many more presumably gave us their preferences. We are distributing this leaflet to give those people more information about the Humanist Party and to introduce the ideals of humanism to others in the community.

Humanism is basically a philosophy that places the human being as the central value in society, rather than money, power, religion or other ideologies. The Humanist Movement is a global organisation working toward the humanization of all countries in the world and the development of the individual as an aware, non-violent person.

In Australia the Movement is represented by the Humanist Party of Australia (HP). While social problems are not as immediately obvious here as they are in many countries, we are still living in a subtly dehumanising society, where most institutions alienate the individual, with poor public participation in government, and where racial, sexual, economic, institutional violence is pervasive.

The HP is working to change this situation in two ways. We are politically active, directly trying to change social conditions. The political awareness of the community and the options for public participation in politics must be developed. This is especially so now, with the current trend towards the conservative political parties.

We also are working on a personal level, encouraging individuals to study the roots of violence within themselves, to become more aware of their position in a global network of humanity, the effects of their actions and their responsibilities. We believe that in order for society to change, we must change our own attitudes, our value systems and the way we relate to others.

New South Wales state election, 19 March 1988.[4]
Legislative Council
<< 1984–1991 >>

Enrolled voters	3,541,447				
Votes cast	3,307,855		Turnout	91.92	–0.60
Informal votes	267,113		Informal	8.01	+1.42
Summary of votes by party					
Party	Primary votes	%	Swing	Seats won	Seats held
Liberal/National Coalition	1,403,300	46.15	+3.54	7	19
Labor	1,140,634	37.51	–9.37	6	21
Call to Australia	174,553	5.74	–0.35	1	3
Democrats	90,634	2.73	–0.42	1	2
Independent EFF	72,965	2.40	+2.40	0	0
Community Independents	52,992	1.74	+1.74	0	0
Environment Group	48,536	1.60	+1.60	0	0
Nuclear Disarmament	28,161	0.93	+0.93	0	0
Aboriginal Team	13,363	0.44	+0.44	0	0
Humanist Party	11.895	0.39	+0.39	0	0
Defence Ex-Service Team	6,970	0.23	+0.23	0	0
Marijuana	2,713	0.09	+0.09	0	0
Independent	3,396	0.11	–0.31	0	0
Total	3,040,742			15	

  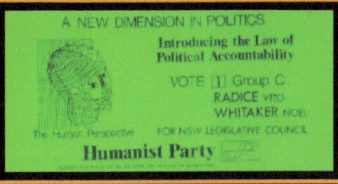

- **Local Council Elections: South Sydney Council- South Ward**
Candidates: Mikey Halliday, Cathie Goudie, Sue Fraser
3rd December, 1988

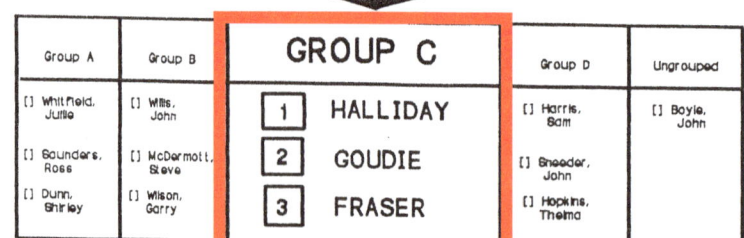

THE NEW BREED
POWER TO THE RESIDENTS
COUNCILLORS NEED TO BE ACCOUNTABLE FOR THEIR POLITICAL ACTIONS

The Humanist Party intends to make South Sydney Council open and accountable to all residents.

A NEW STYLE
The Humanist Party will introduce a new style in the way that council is run and decisions are made.

It is committed to actively promote and consult residents on every major issue and decision made. It will place residents' needs and concerns ABOVE commercial interests.

It will introduce the method of DIRECT DEMOCRACY, in which the council has the function of IMPLEMENTING the decisions made by the residents NOT making decisions.

VOTE 1 HUMANIST PARTY for an OPEN COUNCIL team for the SOUTH WARD in South Sydney Council.

REMEMBER COUNCIL ELECTIONS 3RD DECEMBER.

GROUP "C"

VOTE

1	MIKEY HALLIDAY
2	CATHY GOUDIE
3	SUZANNE FRASER

THE HUMANIST TEAM'S POLICIES:

POLITICAL ACCOUNTABILITY
It is our primary objective to introduce an open and accountable council to the residents of South Sydney and any candidates elected who do not fulfill their election policies will be forced to resign their positions. We will adhere to the following policies:
* Make the council accessible to ALL residents of the municipality.
* Decentralise the council to cater for the needs of samaller areas by dividing the wards into smaller units (precincts).
* No decision will be made about a specific issue unless approved by the RESIDENTS.
* Hold referendums on important issues so that decisions are made by all RESIDENTS.

HOUSING
The housing problem has reached crisis levels all over Sydney and is particularly severe in the inner city.

Rents and house prices have soared beyond the means of ordinary people, particularly youth and disadvantaged.

Urgent measures have to be taken to avoid increasing homelessness. The Humanist Party views affordable accommodation as a RIGHT of every individual.

The Humanist Party will:
* Protect the rights of tenants.
* Introduce a rental limit that is based on a person's weekly income.
* Initiate housing co-operative projects.
* Oppose any destruction of residential dwellings for commercial gain.

YOUTH
More facilities are required within the inner city to cater for the social needs of youth. The H.P. proposes the following:
* Establish Youth Issues as a priority for the council.
* Initiate and develop a Low Rent Youth Housing Scheme.
* Develop and fund Community Youth Job Creation Projects.
* Establish a Youth Cultural Club, offering a variety of recreational and technical activities.
* Initiate and fund Youth Community Arts Projects.

WOMEN
Womens' needs within the municipality have always been overlooked by previous male dominated councils. It's time that womens' views were implemented in real terms.

The H.P. will:
* Initiate a community based support network where all women who suffer ANY problem can go to.
* Open up more womens' health centres within the area.

MIGRANT RESOURCES
In this area the H.P. sees the need to:
* Create more employment for migrant, social, community and youth workers.
* Establish a Multicultural Centre.
* Extend, improve and promote efficient and accessible interpreting services.

CHILDREN'S SERVICES
Children are the future in our society. Special attention is needed to create a safe and secure environment for them to grow in the inner city. The H.P. proposes:
* To provide more quality child care services, including: long day care, after school care, vacation care and 24 hr care.
* Improve recreation facilities for the children in parks, including: upgrading and building skateboard ramps and circuits, cycle tracks and playground equipment.

ENVIRONMENT
The Humanist Party will:
* Oppose the destruction of the environment for commercial gain.
* Make sure all existing green areas are maintained and establish a massive "GREENING" Project.

MEDIA
The H.P. will:
* Support and rehouse 2RSR-FM (Radio Skid Row).
* Support community based media (METRO PUBLIC TV).

TRAFFIC
The H.P. will:
* Make sure that any changes to traffic flow are made with the consultation of all residents involved.
* Promote more efficient public transport thereby reducing the number of vehicles entering the city and the amount carparks required.

WE NEED A NEW PERSPECTIVE IN POLITICS

The Humanist Party (H.P.) is not prepared to allow the direction of our society be determined by politicians whose priorities are continuing their own power monopolies by maintaining a dehumanising society. Why not make a choice for a really different perspective in politics and vote for the Humanist Party.

THE 5 MAIN POINTS OF THE HUMANIST PARTY ARE:
1. The human being must be the central value in society, not money or power.
2. The elimination of all forms of discrimination.
3. The breakdown of monopolies, be they political, economic, ideological or organisational.
4. The development of true co-operative systems in all the processes of society.
5. The use of active non-violence as the only method of action.

FOR MORE INFORMATION PHONE: 799-4601

POLLING BOOTHS FOR SOUTH Sydney Council Elections
South WARD

* Wattle St., Sydney Technical College, Mary Ann St., Ultimo.
* Blackfriars Infants and Nursery School, Blackfriars St., Chippendale.
* Harry Burland Welfare Ctr., Cnr. Ivy and Sheperd St., Chippendale.
* Darlington Public School, Goldengrove St., Darlington.
* Newtown North Public School, Carillon Ave., Newtown.
* Camperdown Demonstration School, 127 Parramatta Rd., Camperdown.
* Uniting Church Hall, King St., Newtown.
* Newtown Public School, Norfolk St., Newtown.
* Erskinville Town Hall, Erskinville Rd., Erskinville.
* Alexandria Public School, Mitchell Rd., Alexandria.
* Waterloo Town Hall, Elizabeth St., Waterloo.
* Waterloo Public School, Botany Rd., Waterloo.
* St. James Church Hall, Collins St., Beaconsfield.
* St. Joseph's School Hall, Rosebery Ave., Rosebery.
* Gardeners Rd. Public School, Gardeners Rd., Rosebery.
* Renwick, Redfern Public School, George St., Redfern.

REMEMBER COUNCIL ELECTIONS 3RD DECEMBER
VOTE [1] GROUP "C" HUMANIST PARTY

HUMANIST PARTY

Authorised by Vito Radica, 36 Parramatta Rd., Summer Hill 2130
Printed by The Humanist Party, P.O. Box 219, Summer Hill 2130

Chapter 8: Rise of the Organisms

Eve of Destruction

"The eastern world, it is explodin',
Violence flarin', bullets loadin',
You're old enough to kill but not for votin',
You don't believe in war, but what's that gun you're totin',
And even the Jordan river has bodies floatin',
But you tell me over and over and over again my friend,
Ah, you don't believe we're on the eve of destruction.

Don't you understand, what I'm trying to say?
And can't you feel the fears I'm feeling today?
If the button is pushed, there's no running away,
There'll be no one to save with the world in a grave,
Take a look around you, boy, it's bound to scare you, boy,
And you tell me over and over and over again my friend,
Ah, you don't believe we're on the eve of destruction.

Yeah, my blood's so mad, feels like coagulatin',
I'm sittin' here, just contemplatin',
I can't twist the truth, it knows no regulation,
Handful of Senators don't pass legislation,
And marches alone can't bring integration,
When human respect is disintegratin',
This whole crazy world is just too frustratin',
And you tell me over and over and over again my friend,
Ah, you don't believe we're on the eve of destruction.

Think of all the hate there is in Red China!
Then take a look around to Selma, Alabama!
Ah, you may leave here, for four days in space,
But when your return, it's the same old place,
The poundin' of the drums, the pride and disgrace,
You can bury your dead, but don't leave a trace,
Hate your next door neighbor, but don't forget to say grace,
And you tell me over and over and over and over again my friend,
You don't believe we're on the eve of destruction.

Performed by: Barry McGuire
Songwriter: P. F. Sloan

It was obvious that action alone was not the right balance! The equilibrium had to be re-established! *"Internal Work"* had to be introduced into weekly meetings and so there was a slight re-adjustment: there was a differentiation made between social/political activities and self-development.

"The Humanist Party" become an *"organism"* launched by *"The Humanist Movement"*. The two would be separate! One could participate in both or just in one of they chose to. One could participate in just *"The Humanist Party"* or they could also choose to participate in *"The Movement"* as well. One could not just participate in "The Humanist Movement"!

Not much later it would drop *"Humanist"* from its name and just be called, *"The Movement"*!

There was another organism launched globally, *"The Greens"*. This was in contrast to the already existing German *"Greens"*!

Here in Australia, "The Greens" already existed, so we launched "The Urban Greens"!

Antonio left Australia to resettle in the UK in February 1988. He now was the Administrator to the highest council, *"Alpha"* which was co-ordinated by *Cobos* and the Support was *Luis Amman*.

Fact Finding Trip to Europe February, 1988:

Antonio soon after suggested that I travel to Europe and experience how the *"The Movement"* was operating in other countries. This was a great idea, so he organised an itinerary and for me to stay with other members.

So in June 1988 I was off to England and Europe.

My trip started in London, Manchester, Glasgow, London, Paris, Milan and then back to London.

What a trip!

It was only for three weeks and it was truly and amazing experience!

The members that I stayed with were complete strangers but they were like we'd been friends for a lifetime beforehand!

We brought this new approach back to Sydney & implemented it straight away!

We had immediate positive results!

It was another fantastic experience and a lot of fun!

From L-R, Glasgow, London, Manchester, London, Milan, Milan

The First International of The Humanist Party, Florence, Italy, 7th January, 1989:

I also was fortunate enough to attend the *"First International of The Humanist Party"* held in Florence on the 7th January 1989.

Mariclaire and I left Sydney on an Air India flight bound for Rome, with short stopovers in Singapore and Mumbai (Bombay) on 3rd January, 1989. About five hours into the flight the plane started to descend, which I thought unusual. I was looking out the window as the plane was landing, I thought, "Singapore has changed, it's all rural!" We in fact had landed in Bali, Indonesia. It was an unscheduled stop. Once on the tarmac, we were told to leave the plane and go into the airport lounge. No one knew what was going on.

Once inside, all the Air India crew disappeared and there was no information given to us and no one to ask what was happening. Air India didn't have an office in Bali! It didn't fly to Bali!

Passengers were becoming frustrated at the lack of information and so some had communication with friends and relatives back in Australia. It was all over the news in Australia, "a threat had been received that an Air India flight bound for Singapore had a bomb on it!"

Us!

This was very scary as a plane had been blown up over Scotland and crashed in Lockerbie on the 21st December, 1988 only a few weeks earlier. Killing everyone on board!

It was a hoax! There was no bomb on board but it did disrupt our travel arrangements. We finally arrived in Florence via Hamburg on a Lufthansa flight from Mumbai on 5th January, 1989, forty eight hours later!

The longest plane flight ever!

The next day, the 6th January, we decided to take a stroll and take in some of the sights of beautiful Florence. However, the city was blanketed in a thick layer of fog. You couldn't see a metre in front of you!

It was sublime!

The Duomo of Florence Cathedral emerged majestically out of the fog as if it was suspended in mid-air!
It was truly transcendental!

As we walked about, we noticed that there was no else about. The streets were all deserted! Where was everyone?

It was mid-morning, going on to lunchtime but not a soul was about?

What the fuck was going?

This was very weird?

All the shops and cafes were also closed!

By this time, we'd been walking for a couple of hours and we were getting peckish so we started looking for a place to have coffee and something to eat. Finally, we found a trottaria that was opened and went in. I asked them in my best Italian, *"Che cazzo sta succedendo oggi? Dove sono tutti? (What the fuck is going on today? Where is everyone?")*. He replied in quite an incredulous tone, *"Non sai cos'è oggi? Oggi, 6 gennaio, è l'Epifania! È un giorno festivo! È uno dei giorni più importanti del calendario cattolico! Tutti sono a casa a festeggiare! (Don't you know what today is? Today, 6th January, is The Epiphany! It's a public holiday! It's one of the most important days in the Catholic calendar! Everyone is at home celebrating!")*.

I felt like a fool!

I'd never heard of "The Epiphany" or the 6th of January as an important day and was a Roman Catholic! Supposedly! It was not celebrated in Australia!

I told him, *"Vengo dall'Australia! Non è celebrato lì! (I come from Australia! It's not celebrated there!")*. With this information he became very excited and told me all about *"l'Epifania (The Epiphany)"*

In Italy, Epiphany is a national holiday and is associated with the figure of "the Befana (la Befana)" (the name being a corruption of the word Epifania), a broomstick-riding old woman who, in the night between January 5 and 6, brings gifts to children or a lump of "coal" (really black candy) for the times they have not been good during the year. The legend told of her is that, having missed her opportunity to bring a gift to the child Jesus together with the Three Wise Men, she now brings gifts to other children on that night.

https://en.wikipedia.org/wiki/Epiphany_(holiday)#Italy

What a wonderful time!

La Befana: The Christmas Witch

Outside, the fog still enveloped the beautiful city of Florence but now we knew that we had it virtually all to ourselves.

What a magical experience!

As we were stolling about, in the thick mist/fog, we were approached by a couple, who stopped and asked us, *"Are you from Australia?"* I answered increduously, *"Yes! But how the fuck did you know that?"*. They answered, *"Who else would be strolling about a deserted Florence on the 6th of January?"*. They were right. The same thing had happened to them. They were also from Australia!
Spooky!
What a small world!

Another amazing thing happened was when we were travelling to Edinburgh, Scotland after Florence and we went past the Lockerbie crash site which was not far from the road. To my astonishment the cockpit of the plane was still there!

Pan Am Flight 103, Lockerbie, Scotland, 21ˢᵗ December, 1988

On January 7th, 1989, the First International of the Humanist Party was held. Thousands of Humanists from around the world joined together to proclaim a world for Humanity. The conference, held in Piazza Santa Croce in Florence Italy was historic as it paid homage to Galileo Galilei.

Below is the text of the inaugural speech given by Afonso Argiolas, the 1st President of the Humanist International Committee.

"I, Galileo Galilei, professor of mathematics of the University of Florence, publically reject my doctrine that the sun is the centre of the world and that it doesn't move, and that the earth is not the centre of the world and that it does move." June 22, 1633.

In 1633, Galileo retracted his statement in order to prevent the same fate as other colleagues. But neither torture nor the stake have stopped courageous men and women from getting hold of a telescope and aiming it, not only in the direction of the stars, but also, in the direction of those who are oppressed and who suffer.

Yet, they, the powerful of the earth, have quickly understood that the new science could be used to nourish their appetite and extend their privileges and thus have educated "a lineage of inventive gnomes", as Bertold Brecht has called them, ready to sell their science to any end and for any price. These intelligent and blind gnomes have found all the ways to join nature to the will of power of their masters and have covered the earth with death machines. Others have used their genius to invent new means of manipulating, silencing and putting the consciousness of the people to sleep.

Undoubtedly, we know other countless men and women have used the new science to alleviate the fatigue and the hunger, the pain and the suffering of humanity, in order to remove the gag from the mouth of the oppressed, in order to give them voice and faith. But we also know that today, as the second millenium of the west comes to an end, the survival of the human species is in danger, and over our own common home, the earth, hovers the nightmare of ecological catastrophe.

It is for this reason that we, humanists from the four corners of the earth, here in front of the building that houses Galileo's tomb, ask for all scientists of the earth to finally use science for the exclusive benifit of humanity.

"Human rights do not have the desired universal scope because they do not depend on the universal power of the human being; rather, they depend on the power that a part has over the whole. They exist in the future, feeding a struggle that comes alive with every new violation of the destiny of mankind. Every demand made in favour of human rights has meaning because it demonstrates to the powers-that-be that they are not omnipotent and that they do not control the future.

Humanists must joint their efforts to better conditions of the world they live in. Wherever dictatorship exists, the humanists will be commited enemies; enemies that will fight until the "mimimum" becomes acceptable... so that the transition from that dictatorship to a formal democracy becomes a fact where a new level of action and proposal can be attained.

Then how could we not decisively support disarmament, which began with the incredible structural revolution of mentality that, since perestroika, and the practice of openess, opens the path towards the ideals of the new society?

What effective methods are being made to impede the death by annihilation of millions of human beings? Which and how many are the effective resourses mobilized and put an end to an asphyxiating and explosive debt in Latin America? In what proportion is the technology needed for development transferred to less favoured zones?

Today it is clear that the world is one; that there are no regions isolated from the whole, and that every catastrophe in one point has repercussions in others. If we try to raise the level of less favoured zones, it will not only be for reasons of solidarity, but also for the survival of human life on the planet--which we consider to be a unity.

Humanist Parties in each place struggle for the following ideal: converting their country to the forefront of a universal human nation. If the particular idea of national parties within a common world project is understood it will be as the full meaning of the proclaimtion "TO HUMANISE THE EARTH."

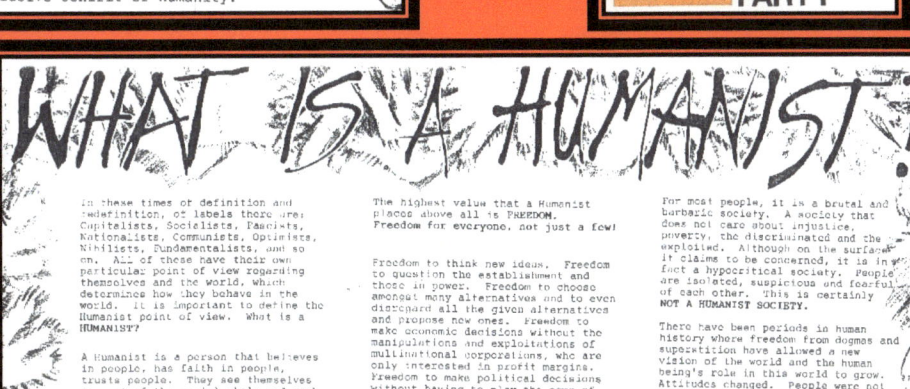

WHAT IS A HUMANIST?

In these times of definition and redefinition, of labels there are: Capitalists, Socialists, Fascists, Nationalists, Communists, Optimists, Nihilists, Fundamentalists, and so on. All of these have their own particular point of view regarding themselves and the world, which determines how they behave in the world. It is important to define the Humanist point of view. What is a HUMANIST?

A Humanist is a person that believes in people, has faith in people, trusts people. They see themselves as part of the social whole and work not only for their own satisfaction but for the wellbeing of the whole society.

This is totally opposed to some attitudes that place individual self-interest as the priority. This in fact, is the prevailing attitude in society today. People are encouraged to think only about themselves, to feed their voracious appetites and not give a damn about the consequences. In this very vicious and brutal world, life of any sort, be it plant, animal or human life, has absolutely no value. The only things that have value are objects and the accumulation of these objects.

A Humanist values equal opportunities for all. These equal opportunities are based on considering certain needs that are fundamental for the wellbeing of all, as basic rights. These are: EDUCATION, HEALTHCARE, HOUSING and EMPLOYMENT.

These basic rights should not be dependent on economic, social or political status of any individual concerned. They should be provided by the whole because they are fundamentally important to life. Without them, people are disadvantaged and, in fact, disabled.

The highest value that a Humanist places above all is FREEDOM. Freedom for everyone, not just a few!

Freedom to think new ideas. Freedom to question the establishment and those in power. Freedom to choose amongst many alternatives and to even discard all the given alternatives and propose new ones. Freedom to make economic decisions without the manipulations and exploitations of multinational corporations, who are only interested in profit margins. Freedom to make political decisions without having to play the game of faking concern about people, when its only some people and vested interests (that of gaining and maintaining power), which are of any concern.

Those that have vested interests to protect, those that are only concerned about themselves have spread the myth that: FREEDOM EQUALS VIOLENCE. This is completely false and the very opposite is in fact correct. IT IS THE DENIAL OF FREEDOM THAT PRODUCES VIOLENCE!

This is the type of society people live in today. It is a society where certain basic freedoms, considered essential for life, are denied to the vast majority of the world's population. It is only a few that have the luxury of being able to satisfy these basic needs. These few are determined not to let these privileges go or to share them with the rest, not easily anyway.

There have been other periods in history very similar to what is experienced in society today. The Middle Ages (or so-called Dark Ages) had a society in which freedom existed for a precious few, the priests and the aristocrats. Those with religious power and those with political power. The rest had absolutely no freedoms whatsoever.

For most people, it is a brutal and barbaric society. A society that does not care about injustice, poverty, the discriminated and the exploited. Although on the surface it claims to be concerned, it is in fact a hypocritical society. People are isolated, suspicious and fearful of each other. This is certainly NOT A HUMANIST SOCIETY.

There have been periods in human history where freedom from dogmas and superstition have allowed a new vision of the world and the human being's role in this world to grow. Attitudes changed. People were not just concerned about their own freedoms but the freedoms of others, of all who made up their community. This new attitude allowed a completely dynamic society to emerge. A society that had a self-confidence not seen before. It was as though the human being had been awakened from a very long sleep. All this was expressed in new forms of technology and culture (philosophy, art, music, politics). This is what is generally called the Renaissance period of human history.

A new Renaissance is required today. A rebirth and a re-awakening of humanity is the answer to the dilemmas that our global society faces today. A lot can be learnt by looking at the past and one of the most basic things that can be learnt is: NOT TO MAKE THE SAME MISTAKES AGAIN. To do this another very valuable lesson can be learnt from observing the past and that is: PEOPLE MUST CHANGE THEIR ATTITUDES. What is needed is a psychological revolution.

To be a Humanist is to have an open mind and not to impose one's beliefs onto others. A challenging task in a world which emphasises the differences amongst people and rewards those that impose their narrow, self-motivated interests onto others, through the use of brute force.

VITO RADICE.

First International of The Green Party, Rio de Janeiro, Brazil on the 7th August 1989:

Cathie, Mariclaire and I were also able to attend *"First International of The Green Party"* was held in Rio de Janeiro, Brazil on the 7th August 1989.

THE GREEN PAPER

REPORT ON THE FIRST INTERNATIONAL GREEN ASSEMBLY

On the 8th July 1989 in the city of Rio De Janeiro, Brazil, representatives of the Urban Greens of Australia, together with two thousand other green members attended the first congress of the GREENS INTERNATIONAL.

There were representatives from 32 countries in all. The countries involved were: Argentina, Australia, Austria, Belgium, Bolivia, Brazil, Canada, Colombia, Chile, Costa Rica, Denmark, Ecuador, Philippines, Finland, France, Greece, Iceland, Italy, India, Mexico, Netherlands, Norway, Panama, Paraguay, Peru, Sweden, Switzerland, United Kingdom, USA, Uruguay, Venezuela and West Germany.

It was a fantastic event! There was an opportunity to talk about global issues in a country where ecological issues are at a catastrophic scale. Especially pertaining to the destruction of the Amazonian rainforest.

There were 8 topics presented which gave a good account of main ecological themes relevant to the global level. These were:
1. The Relationship between the Economy and Ecology at a Global Level.
2. The Demographic Bomb.
3. Energy.
4. The Contaminated Metropolis.
5. World Ecological Emergencies.
6. War Industry.
7. The Dirty Industries of the Multinationals.
8. The Ecological Emergency in Brazil.

The conference elected a co-ordinating body for the Green International. It is composed of 18 members, from various countries, all taking on different functions and being responsible for specific issues. Such as Natural Resources, Human Rights, Ecological Emergencies, Pacifism and Disarmament, Energy and Technology.

Lina De Queiraz (from Brazil) was elected General Delegate of this co-ordinating body. The conference ended with a speech from Lina, referring to the ecological conflicts which are occurring in Brazil. The Amazon was considered as "the lungs of the world". Included in her speech was a profound statement that "the combined interests of a government, a group of landowners, and a handful of multinationals compromise the future of millions of human beings inside and outside Brazil..... the conflict between what's global and what's local begins here".

The Urban Greens of Australia is aware that the only solution to our ecological problems is to actively work on both an international and a local level simultaneously.

It's not enough for people to act in a detached manner without seeing the social and political implications on a larger scale, taking into account the rest of the planet in which we live.

This highlights our major difference between us, the Urban Greens, and other "Green" groups. We are constantly in touch with our international green friends as well as working on specific local ecological issues such as, tree planting, recycling and campaigning for an upgraded free public transport system.

We propose a Green future and a more humane liveable world. Sustainable for future generations.

If you agree with these ideas and our project you are very welcome to join us and become an International Urban Ecologist

Catherine Goudie

International Joint Activity, Paris, August 1990:

Cathie, Mariclaire, Linley and I also went to Paris and London for two weeks in July 1990, to participate in an international week long, joint activity in Paris.

We stayed with Stephane, a member, in his house in Vincennes which is 6.7km east, from the centre of Paris. His parents had gone on a holiday to Israel and so he had the house all to himself. Stephane could speak English very well and probably the reason he was asked to look after us. Which he did magnificently.

The house was a three stories, which in itself was fantastic but what really made extraordinary was that it also had a basement. The basement had a tunnel which connected to *"Vincennes Castle"*. Apparently, the tunnel was used for mistresses and lovers to enter the castle in secret. It was also supposed to be an escape route in case the castle was attacked.

We were organised into groups of about ten people and sent off to various locations throughout Paris to stop people on the street, introduce them to "The Movement", ask them if they were interested and if they were, take them directly to a space that had been hired and another person carried out an "Introductory Meeting", which at the end of, were asked if the wanted to join. This was all done with my almost non-existent French language skills.

The groups consisted of members from all different parts of the globe. It was truly a wonderful experience to interact, participate with all these different nationalities!

The idea was to accelerate the process of participation.

To reduce the time between initial contact & involvement & participation!

"Direct Communication".

A person could be on the street with us, stopping and talking to new people, repeating what they had just experienced, within half an hour!

Stop a person, ask them a couple of simple questions, take them to a locale or coffee shop or any other suitable location, carry out an "Introductory Meeting" which included a simple *"Experience"* (of *Internal Work*) and then ask them to join us on the street, straight away!
No mucking around!

It WORKED!

We brought this new approach back to Sydney & implemented it straight away!

We had immediate positive results!

It was another fantastic experience and a lot of fun!

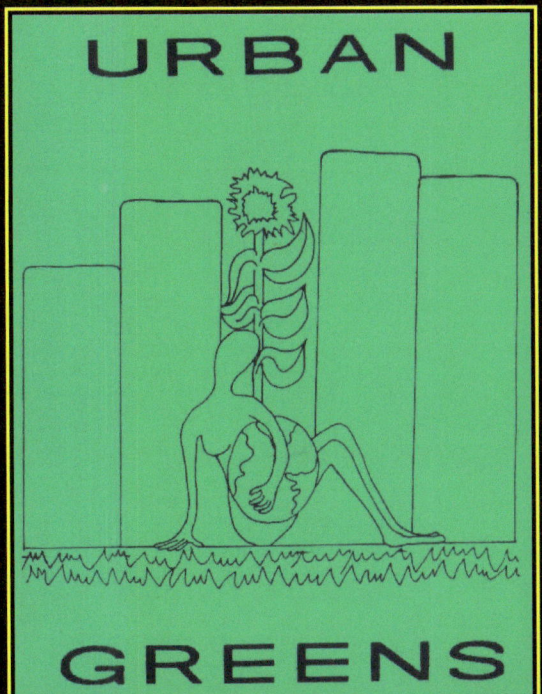

URBAN GREENS

INTRODUCTION

The crisis in which we live in today has a planetary character, one which we are all too familiar with. We live with the anxiety of nuclear war, and the knowledge that half the planet is starving while the other half spends it's time dieting. We live in a country where the gap between rich and poor is widening daily, regardless of whether one is employed or not. It's planetary suicide on the one hand, and on the other it's murder.

Existing politicians and their methods have done little to cure this uneven balance of haves and have-nots. They, unfortunately cannot see beyond their own lifetimes, nor do they wish to see or feel issues smoldering in their own backyards.

The only solution is a global movement. There is more and more consciousness spreading across the globe. People are becoming more aware of the dangers caused by industry and it's waste. More people are realizing the the importance of our natural environment, and it's importance to our wellbeing.

The URBAN GREENS are aware of the issues surrounding conservation and we go beyond. The URBAN GREENS are not just 'a grassroots ecological party'. The URBAN GREENS are also concerned with the urban environment and the issues surrounding it. Issues such as:
* homelessness
* racism
* sexism
* monopolization
* discrimination
* violence

Everything is connected to each and every issue. To approach these issues steps need to be taken to redirect our energies in order to make significant changes in our urban environment.

The URBAN GREENS are a new political party, one which invites ideas and new 'realistic' approaches in order to make changes. We invite you to become a part of the global movement, to work together towards a more human world, for all.

THE URBAN GREENS: THE FORCE OF THE 90'S

1. **AN EQUILIBRIUM BETWEEN PEOPLE AND THE ENVIRONMENT**
    a) The natural environment
    We denounce the destruction of our natural environment which results from the irresponsible stance taken by industrialists who place economic profits before life.
    b) The urban environment
    Our objective is to create a harmony between people and their surroundings. The main concerns are the quality of life, overcrowding, industrial pollution, public health and urban decay in general.
    c) The social environment
    We propose a social environment where it is a basic right of every individual to have an education, good health services, jobs and housing. To develop a true sense of 'community'.
2. **ACTIVE PACIFISM AND DISARMAMENT**
    We propose a progressive disarmament among countries and the redirection of the enormous resources that would result into fundamental areas of need as health, housing, employment and education.
3. **NON-DISCRIMINATION AND PARTICIPATION**
    We are opposed to all forms of discrimination and will overcome this by allowing everyone in the community to be active participants in the decision-making processes.
4. **ECONOMICS BASED ON HUMAN VALUES**
    We support the development of co-operatives and the decentralisation of power and the redistribution of resources.
5. **ACTIVE NON-VIOLENCE**
    Violence generates fear and division among people. The most intelligent method of social change is the use of active non-violence.
6. **SCIENCE AND TECHNOLOGY IN FAVOUR OF LIFE**
    We propose that science and technology be used for the benefit of humanity not for it's destruction.
7. **A NEW APPROACH**
    We propose a new attitude; one of solidarity, freedom and non-violence.

SOME OF OUR POLICIES INCLUDE:

* Strengthen the Environmental Planning and Assessment Act so that all major development must undergo an Environmental Impact Statement, including forestry operations
* All EIS's to be assessed by an independent commission, with much greater opportunity for public input
* The boundaries of National Parks and prohibition of mining in National Parks to be set into the Constitution
* The implementation of the Wilderness Act and the introduction of a Wild and Scenic Rivers Act
* Greater protection for urban bushland and open spaces
* Reduce use of private vehicles in urban areas; upgrading public transport system
* Promote the use of bicycles, build more bicycle lanes
* Convene an "Environmental Summit"
* Undertake massive "greening projects" for the urban environment
* Initiate co-operative housing projects
* Promote the participation of all members of the community in decision-making, especially discriminated groups such as, youth, women, aborigines, migrants and elderly
* Stop all sewage being pumped into open water ways
* Initiate a community based sewage board
* Develop and fund regional community recycling centres
* Stop uranium mining
* Promote a nuclear free and independent Pacific region

FOR MORE INFORMATION ABOUT THE URBAN GREENS CONTACT:

NATHALIE	550-2806
CATHIE	319-2969
NICHOLAS	799-9253

WHY NOT JOIN THE URBAN GREENS?

URBAN GREENS
MEMBERSHIP FORM

NAME...
ADDRESS..
POSTCODE........TELEPHONE.....................
DATE OF BIRTH..../..../....OCCUPATION.................
M/F.....SIGNATURE......................DATE..../..../....

Membership fee is $10.00
Send a cheque or money order made out to:
URBAN GREENS: 6 SUNRISE PLACE, SUMMER HILL 2130

So, who are the URBAN GREENS, and why are they different from other green groups?

The Urban Greens are a political party, operating in local areas working in small grassroots groups. We feel that anyone can start a group and initiate actions within a community, that decision making is possible for any member of our society, not just those who are in a position of power. Although working locally, we keep in contact with other groups in other countries who share our ideals thus being kept aware and in contact with global issues. Above all, we believe in a social ecology where human beings live in a non-violent environment.

If you are interested in finding out more about the Urban Greens please write to us at
P.O. Box 127
ERSKINEVILLE 2043
or contact one of the members listed
Mariclaire 799 4601
Rica 30 1940
Nicholas 799 9253
Cathy 319 2969

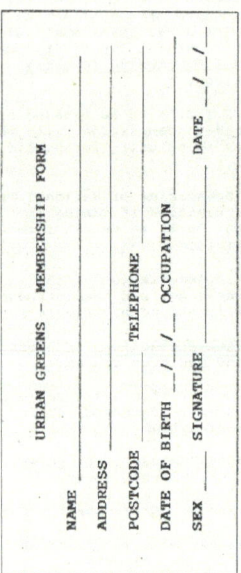

URBAN GREENS - MEMBERSHIP FORM

NAME
ADDRESS
POSTCODE   TELEPHONE
DATE OF BIRTH __/__/__   OCCUPATION
SEX   SIGNATURE   DATE __/__/__

Membership fee is $10.00
Cheques or money orders to be made out to Urban Greens

urban greens

 The crisis in which we live in today has a planetary character, one which we are all too familar with. We live with the knowledge that half the planet is starving while the other half spends its time dieting.

There is more and more consciousness spreading across the globe. The global ecological disasters we now face have been created by people. But the solution to these problems will also come from people. The **Urban Greens** believes that the violence imposed on nature by some human beings is essentially the same violence imposed on other human beings. Much of this violence is generated by a minority of people who have concentrated power- whether it be political, economic or both.

The **Urban Greens** are aware of the issues surrounding conservation but we go beyond. The **Urban Greens** are not just a 'grassroots ecological party'. The **Urban Greens** are also concerned with the urban environment and the issues surrounding it.

Everything is connected to each and every issue. To approach these issues, steps need to be taken to redirect our energies in order to make significant changes in our urban environment.

The **Urban Greens** are a new political party, one which invites ideas and new 'realistic' approaches in order to make changes. We invite you to become part of a global movement, to work together towards a more human world, for all.

SOME OF OUR POLICIES INCLUDE:

* Strengthen the Environmental Planning and Assesment Act so that all major development must undergo an Environmental Impact Statement (E.I.S.), including forestry operations.

* All E.I.S.'s to be assesed by an independent commission, with much greater opportunity for public input.

* The boundaries of National Parks and prohibition if mining in National Parks to be set into the constitution.

* The implementation of the Wilderness Act and the introduction of a Wild and Scenic Rivers Act.

* Greater protection for urban bushland and open spaces.

* Reduce use of private vehicles in urban areas; upgrading public transport system.

* Promote the use of bicycles, build more bicycle lanes.

* Convene an 'Environmental Summit'

* Undertake massive 'greening projects' for the urban environment.

* Initiate co-operative housing projects.

* Promote the participation of all members of the community in decision making, especially discriminated groups such as youth, women, aborigines, migrants and the elderly.

* Find other alternatives to sewrage and waste disposals.

* Initiate a community based sewrage board.

* Develop and fund regional community community recycling centres.

* Stop uranium mining

* Promote a nuclear free and independent Pacific region.

 Here are some of the activites that the **Urban Greens** are involved in;
* tree planting
* lobbying for cycleways in Sydney
* supporting global environmental issues
* cleaning the streets of the inner west
* promoting recycling
* pressuring for more environmentally safe products

WHAT CAN YOU DO?

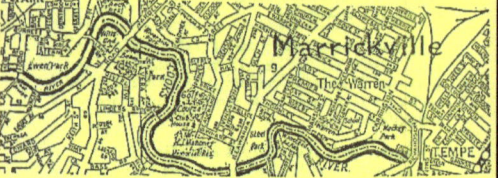
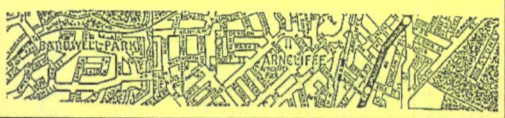

The Law of Political Accountability

Fed up with politicians' broken promises?

Do you have a general mistrust of politicians?
Are you disillusioned with politics in general?
Would you like politicians to stop misleading you?
Would you like politicians to do what they promise?
How can politicians be trusted?
What can be done to make sure that politicians do what they promise?
Shouldn't voters have rights too?

The Humanist Party is campaigning to introduce the
LAW OF POLITICAL ACCOUNTABILITY.

This law would ensure that electoral promises made by a party or a candidate would be binding if elected. It would allow the voters to exercise their democratic right of removing the party from power if the promises are broken.

The Law of Political Accountability is a mechanism which protects the voters from being misled and manipulated by politicians.

The Law of Political Accountability clearly defines the relationship between the voters and the position to be filled.

The Law of Political Accountability lays out the conditions of tenure for the position and the scope of the duties to be carried out.

The Law of Political Accountability is a contract between the voters and the party and/or candidate wishing to be elected. It clearly sets out the responsibilities and what happens if these are broken.

The Law of Political Accountability sets out the rights of voters.

The Law of Political Accountability states:
"The voting public should be able to, at anytime, withdraw their support for a government that is not fulfilling the platform on which it was elected."

1. Political platforms and policies must be presented well before the election for people to study and question.
2. Party platforms and policies (election promises) must contain detailed objectives, methods and time schedules for implementation.
3. These policies will be legally binding documents.
4. If the elected government does not fulfil it's promises a new election can be called through a people's initiated referendum triggered by 10% of the public petitioning parliament.
5. Candidates must sign a contract committing them to the policies of their party, on which they were elected. If they do not represent these policies in parliament, they must resign.

You CAN help!
PHOTOCOPY THE PETITION,
COLLECT AS MANY SIGNATURES AS POSSIBLE
AND SEND TO: The Humanist Party, PO Box 219 Summer Hill 2130.

Petition over page.

The Petition

PETITION
Introduction of The Law of Political Accountability

To the Honourable Speaker and Members of the House of Representatives in the Parliament assembled.

"The voting public should be able to, at any time, withdraw their support for a government that is not fulfiling the platform on which it was elected."

We, the undersigned, demand the introduction of a **Law of Political Accountability**. It states that:

1. Political platforms and policies must be presented well before the election for people to study and question.
2. Party platforms and policies (election promises) must contain detailed objectives, methods and time schedules for implementation.
3. These policies will be legally binding documents.
4. If the elected government does not fulfil it's promises a new election can be called through a people's initiated referendum triggered by 10% of the public petitioning parliament.
5. Candidates must sign a contract committing them to the policies of their party, on which they were elected. If they do not represent these policies in parliament, they must resign.

Your petitioners humbly pray that the House of Representatives call upon the Government to implement the above.

And your petitioners, as in duty bound, will ever pray.

Name	Address	Signature

Chapter 9: Crisis! What Crisis? Scorched Earth

Ruins

It's so quiet in the ruins walking though the old town
Stones crumbling under my feet I see smoke for miles around
Oh it's enough to make you weep, all that remains of the main street
Up in the park on Sunday, dogs chasing and the children played
Old man with his head down, can't see nothing more around, no
But he remembers how it used to be, back in the old days,
So nice to see you coming back in this town again
It's nice to see a friendly face come peeping through having tea
In the afternoon, so nice to see you coming back in this town again
Ah but it's all changed winter turned on a man
Came down on day when no-one was looking and it
Stole away the land, people running scared, losing hands
Dodging shadows of falling sand, buildings standing like empty shells
And nobody...helping no-one else
Young child with his hands high, ain't able to see no reason why, no
But he remembers how it used to be, back in the old days,
So nice to see you coming back in this town again
It's nice to see a friendly face come peeping through
You'd better know what you're going through now
You came back here to find your home is a black horizon
That you don't recognize, evil destruction has taken everything
You'd better walk on the side while you're still walking
Just keep on walking on down the street keep your distance
From the people you meet.
Oh Lord and you'd better watch your eyes
'Cause if smoke gets in them, baby you won't rise again.
Where's it leading to freedom at what cost
People needing more and more and it's all getting lost
I want back, I want back
Back to the time when the earth was green
And there was no high walls and the sea was clean
Don't stop that sun to shine, it's not yours or mine, no.

Songwriter: Cat Stevens

Planet Earth is experiencing enormous environmental pressures unprecedented in human history!

Some still claim that these are natural events NOT that of human making! Clearly, this view is delusional at best and calamitous at worst!

To sit back and do nothing is clearly absurd!

To stand and take action is the most prudent thing to do!

My point of view is that it is better to do everything we can to save the planet rather than to do NOTHING at all!

This was predicted way back in the 60s.

The politicians didn't listen then!

They are not listening still!

I guess they NEVER will!

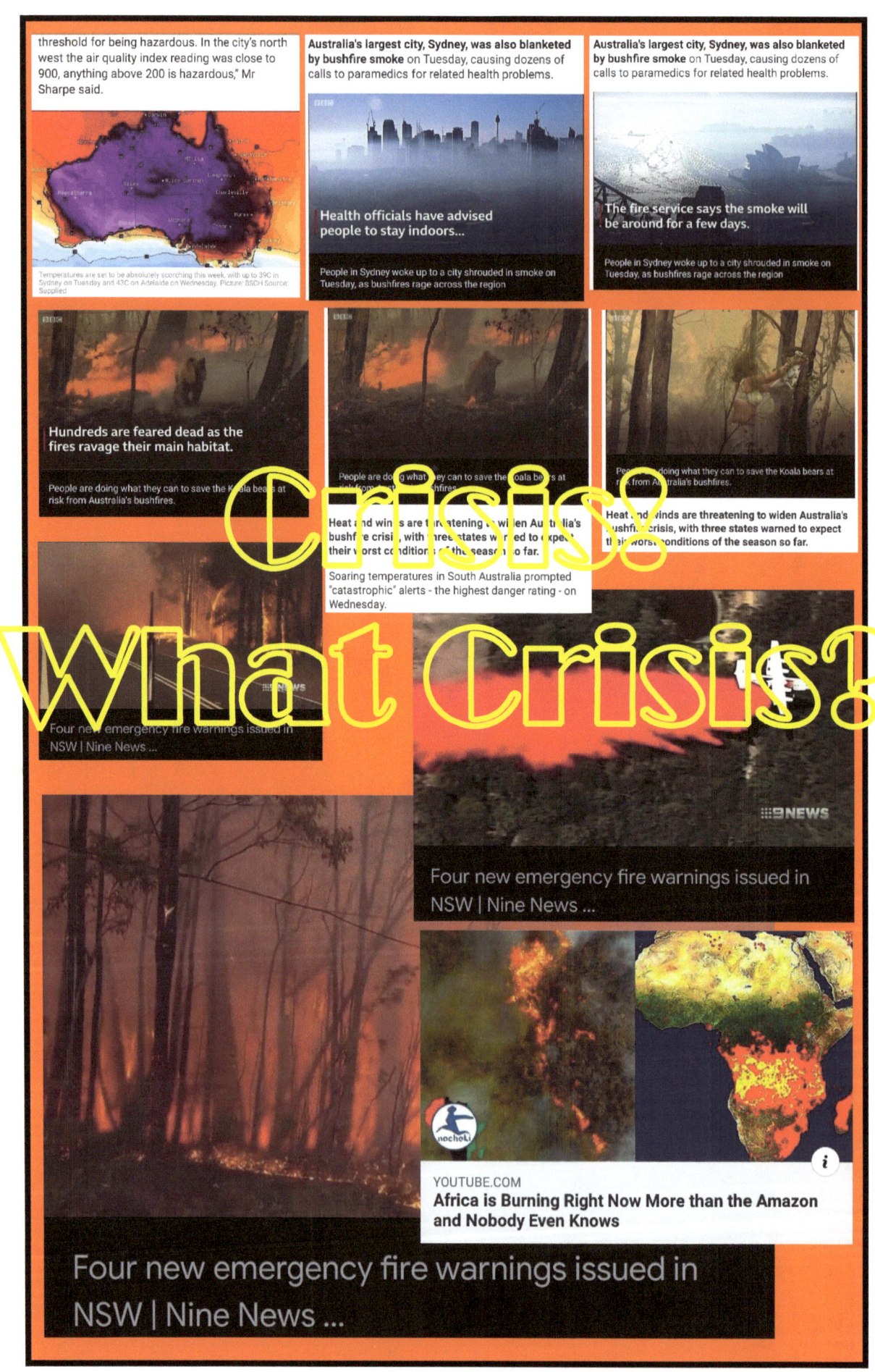

O Caritas

"Hunc ornatum mundi
Nolo perdere
Video flagrare
Omnia res
Audio clamare
Homines
Nunc extinguitur
Mundi et astrorum lumen

Nunc concipitur
Mali hominis crimen
Tristitate et lacrimis
Gravis est dolor
De terraque maribus
Magnus est clamor

O caritas, O caritas
Nobis semper sit amor
Nos perituri mortem salutamus
Sola resurgit vita

Ah, this world is burning fast
Oh, this world will never last
I don't want to lose it
I don't want to lose it
I don't want to lose it, here in my time
Give me time forever
Give me time forever
Give me time forever, here in my time."

Songwriter: Cat Stevens

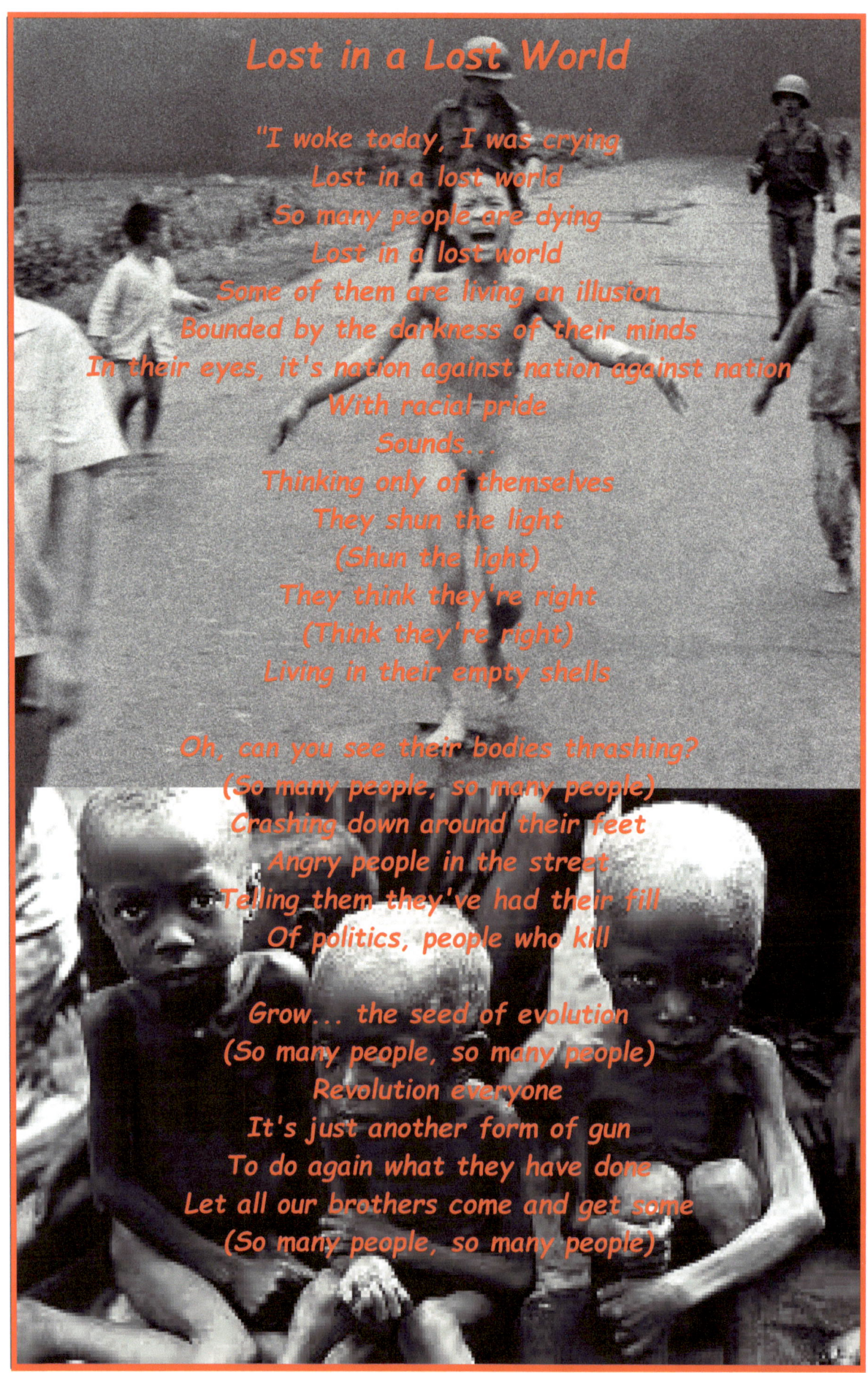

Lost in a Lost World

"I woke today, I was crying
Lost in a lost world
So many people are dying
Lost in a lost world
Some of them are living an illusion
Bounded by the darkness of their minds
In their eyes, it's nation against nation against nation
With racial pride
Sounds...
Thinking only of themselves
They shun the light
(Shun the light)
They think they're right
(Think they're right)
Living in their empty shells

Oh, can you see their bodies thrashing?
(So many people, so many people)
Crashing down around their feet
Angry people in the street
Telling them they've had their fill
Of politics, people who kill

Grow... the seed of evolution
(So many people, so many people)
Revolution everyone
It's just another form of gun
To do again what they have done
Let all our brothers come and get some
(So many people, so many people)

Everywhere you go you see them searching
Everywhere you turn you feel the pain
Everyone is looking for the answers
Well, look again; come on, my friend
Love will find us in the end
Come on, my friend
(On, my friend)
We've got to bend
(Got to bend)
Down on our knees and say a prayer

Oh, can you see the world is pining?
(So many people, so many people)
Pining for someone who really cares enough to share his love
With all of us so we can be
An ever-loving family
Have we forgotten who loves who?
(So many people, so many people)
Children from a family tree
That's longer than a centipede
Started long ago when you and I
Where only love...
(So many people, so many people)

I woke today, I was crying
Lost in a lost world
So many people are dying
Lost in a lost world
So many people, so many people
People lost in a lost world
So many people, so many people
People lost in a lost world."

Performed by: The Moody Blues
Songwriter: Mike Pinder

It's Good News Week

It's good news week
Someone's dropped a bomb somewhere
Contaminating atmosphere
And blackening the sky

It's good news week
Someone's found a way to give
The rotting dead a will to live
Go on and never die

Have you heard the news
What did it say?
Who's won that race?
What's the weather like today?

It's good news week
Families shake the need for gold
By stimulating birth control
We're wanting less to eat

It's good news week
Doctors finding many ways
Of wrapping brains on metal trays
To keep us from the heat

It's good news week
Someone's dropped a bomb somewhere
Contaminating atmosphere
And blackening the sky

It's good news week
Someone's found a way to give
The rotting dead a will to live
Go on and never die

Have you heard the news
What did it say?
Who's won that race?
What's the weather like today?

It's good news week
Families shake the need for gold
By stimulating birth control
We're wanting less to eat

It's good news week
Doctors finding many ways
Of wrapping brains on metal trays
To keep us from the heat
To keep us from the heat
To keep us from the heat

Performed by: Hedgehoppers Anonymous
Songwriter: Jonathan King

Chapter 10: The Journey Ends
End of the Line

End of the Line

Well it's all right, riding around in the breeze
Well it's all right, if you live the life you please
Well it's all right, doing the best you can
Well it's all right, as long as you lend a hand

You can sit around and wait for the phone to ring (end of the line)
Waiting for someone to tell you everything (end of the line)
Sit around and wonder what tomorrow will bring (end of the line)
Maybe a diamond ring

Well it's all right, even if they say you're wrong
Well it's all right, sometimes you gotta be strong
Well it's all right, as long as you got somewhere to lay
Well it's all right, everyday is judgment day

Maybe somewhere down the road aways (end of the line)
You'll think of me, wonder where I am these days (end of the line)
Maybe somewhere down the road when somebody plays (end of the line)
Purple haze

Well it's all right, even when push comes to shove
Well it's all right, if you got someone to love
Well it's all right, everything'll work out fine
Well it's all right, we're going to the end of the line

Don't have to be ashamed of the car I drive (end of the line)
I'm just glad to be here, happy to be alive (end of the line)
It don't matter if you're by my side (end of the line)
I'm satisfied

Well it's all right, even if you're old and grey
Well it's all right, you still got something to say
Well it's all right, remember to live and let live
Well it's all right, the best you can do is forgive

Well it's all right, riding around in the breeze
Well it's all right, if you live the life you please
Well it's all right, even if the sun don't shine
Well it's all right, we're going to the end of the line

Performed by: The Traveling Wilburys
Songwriters: Bob Dylan/George Harrison/Jeffrey Lynne/Roy Orbison/Tom Petty

It was late on a Monday night in February 1992. I had finished a weekly meeting at the Rozelle Neighbourhood Centre with Mariclaire and Cathy. We walked out onto Darling street and I said, "Guys I've had enough! I'm not going to do this anymore!"

And with that, I called it quits on *"The Movement"*!

The race was over.
I gave up!
I walked away from "The Movement", FOREVER!

It is still going on, in one form or another but I never kept in touch!
Hearing bits of information every now and then, such as accidentally bumping into members in Florence, Italy one time, or that *Cobos* had died three years earlier!

I was thirty-two years old!

That was it.........until now, some twenty-eight years later!

Yes, Cobos mythologised himself, and encouraged and perpetuated that myth.

Yes, people idolised him!

Is that necessarily or inherently bad?

Cobos understood very clearly that to create a living organism, a dynamic organisation, to create an identity one has to create "polarity"!

It is a basic law of physics, *"The Law of Duality"*!

Create opposites!
North and south, east and west, good and bad, right and wrong, Ying and Yang, male and female....

That is a fundamental law of nature!

Create a persona, one which can attract some people to you but at the same time, repel others away from you!
This is what he did!
This is what he had to do!
There is NO other way!

Was *Cobos* a good man?
I don't know! I didn't know him personally, intimately, on a human level!

What I do know is that *Cobos* created a world-wide organisation with the aim of making the world a better place!
That, surely is a good thing!
It's good enough for me!

Was it a cult?
Probably!

Did I like it?
Yes!

Was it a positive, life changing experience?
Definitely!

Would I do it again!
Probably!

Would I change anything about it?
Probably!

But that's life!

Cobos attempted an amazing feat, one that very few people attempt!

That, in itself is an amazing thing!

I learned a great deal from being involved!

It has shaped my life ever since. It is the basis of all my thinking, values & beliefs that I have about myself and society!

Everything I do, is based on those ideas!

I am whom, I am because of *"The Movement"*!

In my own way, I am still doing what *Cobos* set out to do all those years ago: to change oneself and the world and make it better! A better person, a better world!

If you're gonna join a cult, make sure it's a good one!

It's no coincidence that cult is found in the word *"CULTure"*!!

Is *"culture"* one big cult?
The cult of *"Humanity"*!

Did I fail?

Did we fail?

NO!

Our so called *"Leaders"* HAVE failed us!
They have lied!
They have cheated!
They are selfish!
They are arrogant!
They manipulate!
They deceive!
They are corrupt!
They do not value life of any sort!
They used & abused us!
They value power!
They lack humanity!
They are PSYCHOPATHS!

We have not failed!
We still have our HUMANITY!
We will succeed!
There is no other outcome!

Did I have a choice?

No!

Being the person that I was and am, there was NO other choice!

The path was clear & well defined!
There was no other outcome!

Consciousness ALWAYS wins!
There is NO alternative!

What were the most valuable ideas that I learnt?

On a personal level, probably the most valuable knowledge that has been the most useful for me is *"The Theory of Impulses"*, how images are charged in the Consciousness and control human behaviour.

Being able to charge and discharge images is the act of *"Intentionality"*!

You can either be a cork in the river & just go along for the ride (Mechanicity/Determinism) or you can control where you want to go (Intentionality)!

The recognition of this fact is *"Self- awareness/Self-observation"*!

Politically would have been *"The Law of Political Accountability"*. The Humanist Party was talking about this as early as 1986 and it is now more relevant than ever.
People are enormously disillusioned with politicians and rightly so! They need to be held accountable! There has to be consequences about the promises they make & when they don't deliver! Which is basically all the time and by all politicians from the whole political spectrum, left, right and anywhere in between!

Ultimately, I believe that we don't need politicians to represent us and should get rid of them, but that's another story!

Ok a clue, "Direct Democracy"!

> *"My friends, even when we do not immediately achieve the results that we have hoped for, this seed exists already, and awaits the arrival of the times that are to come.*
>
> *For all, from heart to heart, the fervent desire for this coming social change and the hope for this silent transformation which, beyond all compulsion, beyond all impatience, beyond all violent aspiration, beyond all guilt and all feelings of failure, is already nesting in the intimate depths of many humanists."*
> *Extract of a talk by Cobos given on the 4th of January 1998 in the Obras Sanitarias stadium in Buenos Aires, Argentina*
>
> http://www.humanistmovement.net/

Not The End

Road to Somewhere

Well we know where we're going
But we don't know where we've been
And we know what we're knowing
But we can't say what we've seen
And we're not little children
And we know what we want
And the future is certain
Give us time to work it out
Yeah

We're on a road to somewhere
Come on inside
Taking that ride to somewhere
We'll take that ride
I'm feeling okay this morning
And you know
We're on the road to paradise
Here we go, here we go

We're on a ride to somewhere
Come on inside
Taking that ride to nowhere
We'll take that ride
Maybe you wonder where you are
I don't care
Here is where time is on our side
Take you there, take you there!

We're on a road to somewhere!
We're on a road to somewhere!
We're on a road to somewhere!

There's a city in my mind
Come along and take that ride
And it's alright, baby, it's all right
And it's very far away
But it's growing day by day and it's all right
Baby, it's all right
Would you like to come along
You can help me sing the song
And it's all right, baby, it's all right
They can tell you what to do
But they'll make a fool of you
And it's all right, baby, it's all right

There's a city in my mind
Come along and take that ride
And it's alright, baby, it's all right
And it's very far away
But it's growing day by day and it's all right
Baby, it's all right, yeah
Would you like to come along
You can help me sing the song
And it's all right, baby, it's all right
They can tell you what to do
But they'll make a fool of you and it's all right
Baby, it's all right

We're on a road to somewhere!
We're on a road to somewhere!
We're on a road to somewhere!
We're on a road to somewhere!

Original song entitled; "Road to Nowher" Performed by: Talking Heads
Songwriters: Chris Frantz/David Byrne/Jerry Harrison/Tina Weymouth
(with apologies to Talking Heads)

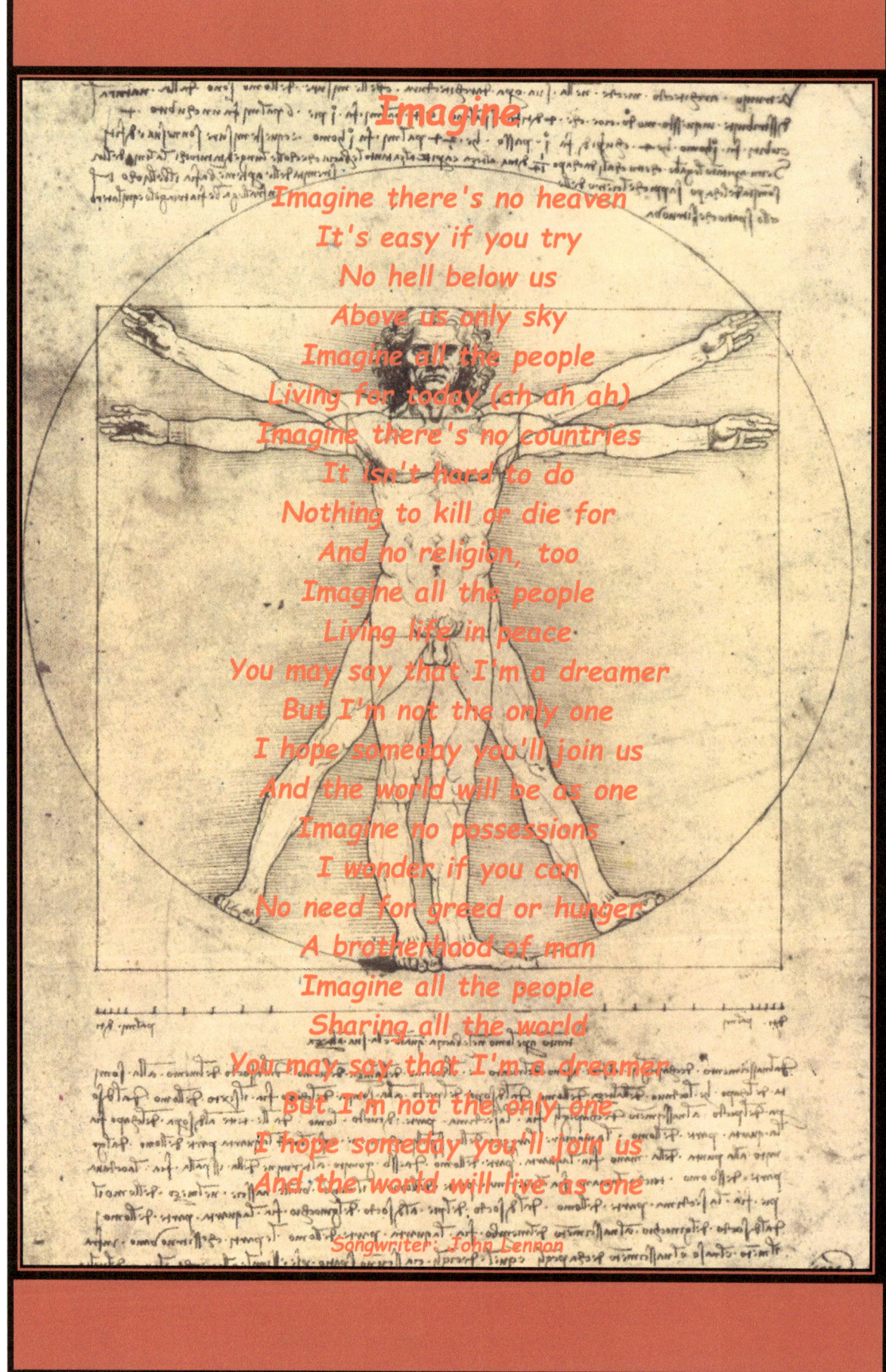

Imagine

Imagine there's no heaven
It's easy if you try
No hell below us
Above us only sky
Imagine all the people
Living for today (ah ah ah)
Imagine there's no countries
It isn't hard to do
Nothing to kill or die for
And no religion, too
Imagine all the people
Living life in peace
You may say that I'm a dreamer
But I'm not the only one
I hope someday you'll join us
And the world will be as one
Imagine no possessions
I wonder if you can
No need for greed or hunger
A brotherhood of man
Imagine all the people
Sharing all the world
You may say that I'm a dreamer
But I'm not the only one
I hope someday you'll join us
And the world will live as one

Songwriter: John Lennon

In Memory of Tom Torok

I met Tom in January 1983 in Hyde Park, Sydney. Sydney City Council had organised a "Peace Week" and had sectioned off a corner of the park for community and peace groups to up set up stalls and organise activities to engage with people.

It was a fantastic initiative and something which should be encouraged and organised again. It was a fantastic week! Tom immediately become involved and remained an active long after I had left.

I had not seen Tom nor did I keep in touch but one evening I received a phone call from another member telling me that Tom was very sick in hospital and that he was going to die very soon and that he wanted to see me.

I was in shock! I began to cry.

Tom had pancreatic cancer and was told that he only had a few days left to live. I rushed to St Vincent's Hospice where he was in palliative care. There was nothing doctors could do for him anymore. He had come to the end of his journey.

He had lost a lot of weight and no longer looked like the Tom I knew all those years ago, but he looked great and at peace with himself. He could still walk around and we went into the sitting room and we talked for about an hour.

I hugged and left him.

He died two days later.

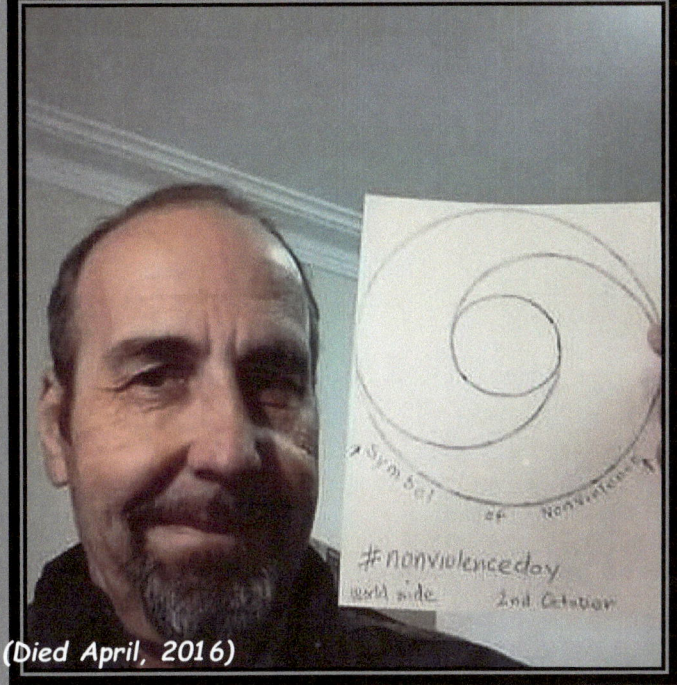

(Died April, 2016)

Heroes

I, I will be king
And you, you will be queen
Though nothing will drive them away
We can beat them, just for one day
We can be heroes, just for one day

And you, you can be mean
And I, I'll drink all the time
'Cause we're lovers, and that is a fact
Yes, we're lovers, and that is that

Though nothing will keep us together
We could steal time, just for one day
We can be heroes, forever and ever
What d'you say?

I, I wish you could swim
Like the dolphins, like dolphins can swim

Though nothing, nothing will keep us together
We can beat them, forever and ever
Oh, we can be heroes, just for one day!

Written & performed by: David Bowie

My best friends & fellow collaborators, whom I owe an enormous debt of gratitude, Mariclaire, Sue & Nyoka.
Thank you guys.
"The Don"

www.ingramcontent.com/pod-product-compliance
Lightning Source LLC
Chambersburg PA
CBHW041430010526
44107CB00046B/1564